1990

IF YOU ARE RAPED:

What Every Woman Needs To Know

Consulting Editor

Human Services Series

Edsel L. Erickson

Western Michigan University

IF YOU ARE RAPED:

What Every Woman Needs To Know

Kathryn M. Johnson

LP **Learning Publications, Inc.**
Holmes Beach, FL 33509

Johnson, Kathryn M., 1952-
    If you are raped.

    Bibliography: p.
    Includes index.
      1. Rape—United States.   2. Rape victims—United
States.   3. Rape victims—Services for—United States.
I. Title.
HV6561.J64 1985   362.8'8   83-83181
ISBN 0-918452-72-4

Copyright 1985 Kathryn M. Johnson

Learning Publications, Inc.
P.O. Box 1326
Holmes Beach, FL 33509

Printing: 1 2 3 4 5 6 7 8   Year: 5 6 7 8 9

Printed in the United States of America

Acknowledgment

This book would not have been possible without the many women who were willing to share their fears, concerns and reactions to the crime of rape. Although they remain nameless, they are neither forgotten nor unrecognized.

Many others have helped in the production of this work including: Steve Kuemmerle, Danna Downing, Gayle Govert, Laura Johnson-Manis, Edsel Erickson, Alan McEvoy and Jeffrey Brookings, the Johnson's, Jan Conklin, Michael Manis, Kathy and Tim Middleton, Susan Caringella-MacDonald, Paula Neff, Joseph Pellicciotti, Marty Zusman, Dianna West, Emily Hollenberg, David Barch, Andrea Stoller, Regina McGraw, and the Kuemmerle's. Thank you, all.

For Eli

Table of Contents

If you have ever been raped,
this book is for you.

If you fear being raped,
this book is for you.

If you want to be prepared in case you are raped,
this book is for you.

If you want to help lessen
the burden of rape for all women,
this book is for you.

1

What is Rape?

Rape is a crime which affects us all, every day of our lives. In this book, we will examine why rape occurs, how it can be prevented and, most importantly, what to do if you are raped. The health and well-being of all rape victims depend upon what they do and think after the rape occurs. This book will help you understand those behaviors, thoughts and feelings. If you are raped, it will also help you learn how to get valuable counseling, medical care and legal assistance.

What Do We Mean By Rape?

The U.S. Federal Bureau of Investigation presently defines rape as follows:

> Forcible rape is the carnal knowledge of a female forcibly and against her will. Assaults or attempts to commit forcible rape by force or threat of force are also included. . . .

This is an incomplete definition of rape. In fact, because rape is so often narrowly defined, many women do not know what constitutes the crime. Is it only forced intercourse? Is it rape only if it is committed by a stranger? Is it rape if the victim does not fight back? Answers to these questions are not apparent in most definitions of rape, including the one given above. Moreover, beyond being incomplete, legal definitions of rape do not remain constant. They vary greatly from country to country, and region to region.

However, regardless of legal differences, for our purposes:

Rape is any sexual act that is attempted or completed by force, threat of force or coercion against another person's will.

We will examine this definition more closely.

- Rape occurs any time a sex-related act is forced upon another person. This includes everything from fondling or oral sex to actual intercourse. Even forcing a person to disrobe and be stared at or photographed is included in this definition. Sexual acts that do not include the rapist's genitalia (but rather hands, mouth or some instrument) are also included.

- Rape involves the use of force or threat of force. Anytime a victim is forced or coerced to the point of physical *or* emotional powerlessness, rape has occurred. Even if the victim does not fight back, force or threat of force is all that is necessary for rape to occur.

- Rape includes attempted as well as completed acts. Simply being placed in the position of fearing rape, even if the rape is not completed for some reason, constitutes the crime of rape.

- Rape may be committed against any person. Rape is not a crime that necessarily strikes any one group of victims. Young and old, black and white, male and female—anyone can be raped. Rape is violent sexual abuse against another person, regardless of who that person is or what that person does with her or his life.

This book is written for all victims and potential victims of rape. It is especially written for female victims. This is not meant to imply that men cannot be raped; they often are. However, the rape of men is by far more rare than the rape of women. Primarily, it is women who have suffered the burden of rape over the centuries. As such, the needs of women rape victims, and women who live in fear of rape, deserve the special attention they receive in this book.

- Rape is sexually-related, rather than sexually-motivated. There is a fine, and often confusing, line between these distinctions. Rape is not an expression of sexual desire on the part of the rapist. Rather, it is violence expressed through sexual activity. Rape is neither sex nor lovemaking; it is violence. The questions and controversy surrounding the sexual motivations of rapists will be discussed more fully in the next chapter.

What women mean when they say the word "rape," and how rape is defined by law, can therefore be quite different. For example, in the place where you live, the legal definition of rape may include only sexual intercourse and not sexual fondling or touching. However, regardless of such limited legal definitions, women know when they have been raped. If you have had a sexual act committed against you without your consent, or if you fear such acts, you know exactly what rape means.

It should be pointed out that today the word "rape" is often replaced by other terms. Many believe that the word rape is too limiting a term—implying only forced intercourse by a man against a woman. We increasingly hear terms such as sexual assault, sexual misconduct, sexual aggression, forced sexual aggression, forced sexual activity and so forth. In this book, the word rape is used to include *every* kind of forced sexual behavior.

How Often Does Rape Occur?

Unfortunately, rape occurs much more often than any of us would like to think. Thousands and thousands of women are raped each year. Moreover, it may be that rape is becoming increasingly common. It certainly appears that way when one examines crime statistics. Each year, more rapes are reported to the police than the year before. This may be due to the fact that more women are willing to report rape in this day and age. Or, it may be that more women are actually being raped. We have no way of knowing for certain which is the case. What we do know is that even one rape a year is one too many.

The U.S. Federal Bureau of Investigation noted 82,088 reported rapes and attempted rapes in 1980. If unreported rapes were included in this figure, a much higher number would probably be more accurate. For example, a 1982 survey taken by the U.S. Bureau of the Census showed that 192,000 persons indicated that they had been the victims of rape. Of this number, only 50.5% were reported to the police. Regardless of how rapes are counted, the final tally remains horribly high. Women are angry and frightened. They are demanding that changes be made to reduce this staggering figure.

How Can This Book Help?

It has been said that understanding is the key to change. This book will help you to understand the crime of rape. But it will also do more. This book will help you to:

- Know how to avoid being raped.

- Cope with being raped.

- Face your friends, family and co-workers if you are raped.

- Find the kinds of services that are available to rape victims.

Suggestions provided in this book offer practical advice based upon the experience of other rape victims, those who have helped them recover and those who have devoted their lives to the study of this crime. Today, more and more people are examining what it means to be raped. This attention means that we know more about the crime of rape than ever before. New laws and punishments, the retraining of professionals and the organization of rape crisis centers across the country are all helping to lessen the problems of those who suffer rape. This book summarizes these improvements and presents them to everyone who is concerned with rape. As horrible as the crime of rape is, it can be overcome and someday, hopefully, completely eliminated.

2

Why Rape Occurs

The study of rape is extremely complicated. A great many issues surround the crime: cultural learning, psychological problems, legal definitions and victims' attitudes, to name but a few. There are no easy explanations for why rape occurs. We are confused by the complexity of the crime. It would be impossible to explain rape with one simple statement.

Despite these problems, tremendous progress is being made in the study of rape. It is as if all the thousands of pieces of a jigsaw puzzle are starting to converge into a recognizable picture. As more and more people think about, discuss and study the crime of rape, our puzzle becomes more complete. We still have a long way to go before rape is totally understood. We are closer today, however, than ever before.

The most important reason for this current level of understanding is to be found in the increased attention directed toward the crime of rape. Contemporary insight is leading to a change in attitudes and knowledge about who is likely to be raped, who is at fault and why rape occurs. As we examine where we stand today on this issue, in comparison to our historical stance, we see that many harmful myths about rape are being reconsidered. Age-old notions about the crime of rape are slowly disappearing. Damaging myths such as ''women want to be raped'' or ''women deserve to be raped'' are finally being dispelled as we add to our knowledge.

It must be remembered that these and other myths about rape have solid roots in ancient history. To illustrate this, we can travel back to ancient Babylonia. The Babylonian legal structure, the Code of Hammurabi, decreed that if a married woman were raped, both she and her rapist would be punished by being put to death. In the eyes of the law, the victim was every bit as much to blame as her attacker. (The only women who were safe under this code were young virgins who were viewed differently. They were not seen as being at fault for the rape. Thus began the separation of treatment for "good" women and "bad" women, a separation which, as we will see, remains today to some extent.)

Throughout the ages, rape continued to be viewed as a special kind of crime, if a crime at all. History tells of war time rape, when conquering heroes raped women in enemy countries as their "due reward." (Some historians suggest that raping women during war time provided a means by which soldiers could assume power, thereby making up for any perceived weaknesses on the battlefield.) The underlying assumption was, of course, that a man had the right to take any woman who happened along simply because he was her master, entitling him to any type of control over her that he wanted—even violent control.

Unfortunately, these perceptions remained with us into the twentieth century. Only now are we beginning to reconsider our damaging and faulty historical traditions.

Our recent changes in attitudes and knowledge have led to some improvements in the treatment of rape victims. No longer must women be treated as "criminals" if they are raped. Legal and medical institutions, families and friends, as well as victims themselves, are beginning to understand that rape is never the victim's fault.

We have a long way to go before rape is in its proper place as a criminal activity. (For example, the Code of Hammurabi is still reflected in the laws which allow a man to rape his wife because she is considered his property.) Nonetheless, vast improvements have been made. Such improvements are reflected in changing attitudes and laws that govern the crime of rape.

Myths About Rape

The crime of rape cannot continue to be colored by traditional myths, false assumptions and inaccurate attitudes. What are these myths, and how have we come to know that they are false? We will first discuss these myths in contrast to recently acquired knowledge about the crime of rape. The laws regarding rape will be explored later in Chapter 10.

Myth: Rape is an expression of intense sexual desire.

Fact: Rape is an expression of some men's need to dominate women.

Many people mistakenly believe that men who rape do so because of a biological need for sexual release and gratification. It is as if a physical time bomb goes off, demanding immediate sexual satisfaction. *Rape is not an act of sexual need.* Rather, it is an expression of violence and domination. In fact, many rapists have normal and active sex lives with wives or lovers. In areas where prostitution is readily available for sexual release, rape is still a problem. This is because rape is motivated by a totally different, non-sexual need; the need to dominate, control and degrade women. Men who rape consider women to be "fair-game," to be taken at will. Women become their possessions, subject to their need for violence.

> . . .rape serves essentially nonsexual needs in the psychology of the offender. Rape is not primarily the aggressive expression of sexuality but rather the sexual expression of aggression (Groth, 1983, p. 1352).

Research has shown that aggression is triggered by feelings of anger or violence, or by a rapist's need to control and dominate another person, or by both. Some rapists hurt and punish their victims out of a need to release pent-up anger and frustration, others have deep feelings of inadequacy that are relieved by being able to dominate and control another person. Study of how rapists view themselves has shown that most display aggression due to a low self-concept, doubts about their manhood, a feeling of being socially distant or a general unhappiness with their lives. Few, if any, state that they derive any particular sexual satisfaction from rape.

Moreover, it has also been shown that up to one half of all rapists are sexually dysfunctional during the rape. This means that they are unable to achieve erection, or that they exhibit either premature ejaculation or no ejaculation at all. These same rapists report no sexual difficulties when they are engaged in consenting sexual relationships. Many rapists also state that during the rape they feel no sense of sexual stimulation or arousal.

Some people view the position stated above as too extreme in its rejection of sexual motivation as a cause of rape. Such a viewpoint is demonstrated by recent court decisions in which convicted rapists were sentenced to castration or drug therapy programs designed to reduce or counter-balance their male sex hormone (testosterone) levels. The assumption is that some men rape due to uncontrollable sexuality caused by elevated testosterone. It is assumed that if their hormone levels could be lowered (through castration or drug therapy) the "need" to rape would cease. Further, it is assumed that the castrated rapist, made incapable of sexual intercourse, would also be incapable of rape. However, despite these assumptions, *careful research has not been able to establish any significant connection between true sexual desire on the part of the rapist and the motivation to rape.*

It is not at all certain whether castration is effective in preventing rapists from repeating their crimes. There are many examples of cases where convicted and castrated rapists continue to display violent behavior. Some go on to rape again, using broomsticks to replace their severed organs. A great number of rapes take place with various implements used in place of the penis even by men who are not castrated. Furthermore, the loss of sexual potency by rapists who have been castrated can result in a deep sense of bitterness and anti-social behavior leading to increased violence. In California during the 1940's, many sexual offenders were sentenced to castration. While no carefully controlled studies of these offenders were performed, many of the castrated men were reported to remain violent after castration.

On the other hand, some changes toward reduced violent behavior have been observed among castrated rapists in Europe. It should be pointed out, however, that these rapists also received mandatory, extensive professional counseling. As such it is not clear whether the counseling, or the castration, resulted in the reduced expression of violence.

It should also be noted that some rapes are committed by women. Obviously, these rapes stem from causes other than the possession of male sexual organs.

The extent to which rape occurs due to an increased level of testosterone in a rapist's body is also not clear. Testosterone, normally present in all people, has been shown to be responsible for many normal male characteristics (growth of facial hair, deepening of the voice at puberty, muscular distribution throughout the body and so forth). Some studies show that some rapists have higher than normal testosterone levels. This has been used as a justification for the use of drugs to reduce testosterone levels in rapists in order to reduce the recurrence of the crime. These studies are inconclusive for a number of reasons:

- Increased testosterone has been associated with an increase in aggressive behavior. However, it has not been proven whether the increased testosterone levels are associated with rape.

- It is uncertain whether increased testosterone causes increased aggression, or if the distress leading to aggression also causes an increase in testosterone levels. In other words, the displayed aggression of rapists may be caused by social factors, and elevated testosterone levels are simply the result of such distress.

- Many men who display no particular violent or aggressive behavior, and who show no inclination toward rape, have elevated testosterone levels.

Finally, remember that both men and women have sex drives. Yet, it is men who perpetrate the vast majority of all rapes. This alone suggests that the cause of rape must lie primarily in the nature of our culture, and not within the characteristics of our biology.

Myth: Rape is a part of human nature.

Fact: Rape is learned behavior.

The evidence for this comes from the fact that not all cultures have the same incidence of rape. For example, many industrialized nations have far lower rape rates than the United States. In some cultures, rape does not even exist. In a study of the Arapesh, Margaret Mead discovered that Arapesh men knew nothing about rape, even though they had heard of it occurring elsewhere. They did not understand how such a thing could be possible. This serves to illustrate the fact that rapists learn to rape. If this were not so, "human nature" would dictate that at least some Arapesh men would rape. Despite our many cultural and regional differences, humans are all one species. If rape were a part of "human nature," rape would be a trait of our species and all cultures of the world would have their rapists. The fact that this is not so eliminates this possibility.

Myth: Rape is a lonely man's response to a lack of love.

Fact: Rape is neither an act of sex nor an act of love. Rape is an act of violence.

Many psychologists and other social scientists believed for a long time that rapists were lonely men looking for affection. According to this assumption, men just wanted temporary closeness with women. The image of the homely or plain man, continually rejected by women, was a popular stereotype of the "typical" rapist. Rape, however, is an act of violence, not affection. Rape almost always includes the use of force or threat of force. Well over one third of all rapes involve the threat or use of deadly weapons. Many victims are injured by their rapists in a variety of ways, beyond sexual and emotional injury. Most rapists show a history of violent activity, many with prior records for violent assaults. Rape is likely to be an act of anger and frustration and the need to dominate. It is not an expression of love.

Myth: Rapes always occur spontaneously.

Fact: Rapes are quite often carefully planned and executed.

This myth is similar to the first myth which suggests that some men suddenly explode and immediately demand a sexual partner. Actually, rape is often a premeditated behavior, based on well thought out plans for domination and control. Many rapists take the time to plan the rape scenario, obtain a weapon and choose a suitable location for the rape. In some cases, rapists acquaint themselves with their would-be victims before they actually attack.

Myth: A rapist is mentally ill.

Fact: A rapist can be any man.

Perhaps no one issue has caused quite as much controversy and debate as whether or not rapists are mentally ill, deranged or somehow different from the rest of the population. Certainly no one could dispute the fact that the act of rape is "sick." However, are rapists themselves sick individuals who cannot help what they do? Many people thought so throughout much of our history. Today, this belief is being disputed. Research is showing that only a very small percentage of known rapists can be classified as seriously mentally ill. Most rapists do not appear to be unique or psychotic. What is common to all rapists is a need to dominate women; to be in charge. Rapists are not noticeably different from non-rapists in terms of promiscuity, appearance or behavior. One rape counselor reports working with a group of rapists including doctors, lawyers, priests and other professionals. There is no way to predict accurately who will rape.

Myth: Rape is usually committed by a man of one race against a women of another race (interracial rape).

Fact: Most rapes are committed within one racial group (intraracial rape).

Actually, two quite similar myths abound regarding interracial rape. One is that black rapists are inclined to choose white women as their victims; the other is that white rapists choose black women as their preferred victims. What we see is that each race views the other with distrust and fear. In truth, the majority of all rapes are committed by men who are of the same race as their victims.[1]

Although interracial rape is not typical, it does occur. When one examines rape statistics (as they are recorded by the police,) it appears as if interracial rape is primarily a case of a black rapist against a white victim. If unreported rapes are included in the analysis, however, a quite different pattern emerges.

---

[1] It was once thought that interracial rape accounted for less than ten percent of all rapes. Some more recent research shows that interracial rape may be slightly higher than that, at least in some parts of the country.

Then white rapist/black victim rapes appear to be equally common. This is due, in part, to the dramatic underreporting of rape by black victims, especially if their rapist is white. It is believed by many black victims that the legal establishment will take no action against white rapists.

It is true that black rapists (of white women) are more harshly treated than are white rapists (of black women). White rapists are less likely to be arrested and convicted for their crimes. Moreover, black rapists are much more likely to be arrested and convicted if their victims are white. In other words, the laws are more strictly enforced for the protection of white women from black rapists, than for the protection of black women from either white or black rapists.

Another problem with the issue of interracial rape is that its proportions are easily magnified by statistics. The reason is as follows:

1. Interracial rape is usually committed by men unknown to their victims (i.e., stranger rape).

2. We know for certain that stranger rape is reported to the police more frequently than is acquaintance rape (i.e., the rapist is known to the victim, such as a friend or a lover).

3. We also know that acquaintance rape is almost always committed by and against people of the same race. Therefore, if we were to include all of the unreported, intraracial acquaintance rapes in our statistics, the actual percentage of stranger, interracial rapes would be dramatically minimized.

In summary, most rapes are committed by men who are of the same race as their victims. If all rapes were reported, it is quite likely that we would see a very small percentage of interracial rape. That small percentage would be equally comprised of both black rapist/white victim and white rapist/black victim cases.

Myth: Some women secretly desire to be raped.

Fact: Women view rape as a terrifying experience.

Unfortunately, a great many people mistakenly believe that there are women who secretly long to be taken against their will. This has certainly been a popular theme in books and movies. However, women know that the act of rape is a horrifying and life-threatening experience. Women do not accept the crime of rape. Some try to fight off their attackers, others are frozen with terror throughout the event. No woman wants to be used and threatened against her will.

Certainly many women fantasize about being "swept off their feet" by a loved one or a handsome stranger. However, such fantasizing should never be perceived as secret desire to be raped. The two are totally separate. Even women who dream of or enjoy being told what to do sexually are engaging in behavior that allows them a degree of control and trust. This is *not* the case in the crime of rape.

Myth: Some women "deserve" to be raped.

Fact: Rape is a crime to which no woman should be subjected.

A woman may be raped regardless of her appearance or actions. Men do not rape only those whose outward appearance or behavior might be judged by some to be sexy, loose or attention-getting. Elderly women and infants are raped. It does not matter whether a woman is single or a wife and mother; whether she works in a tavern or is a school teacher; whether she wears sexy or conservative clothing—*no woman deserves to be raped.*

Myth: A man rapes a woman because she ''asks for it'' by being careless.

Fact: Regardless of where a woman is, no one has the right to rape her.

A woman who walks alone, or goes out for a drink, does not ''deserve'' to be raped any more than a store with only one lock ''deserves'' to be robbed. Certainly everyone in modern society takes some precautions. However, precautions alone do not provide insurance. Many women are raped in their own homes, others while out alone. No woman is responsible for the behavior of a rapist merely because she happens to be in any given place, at any given time, or with any given person. Comments like, ''What did she think would happen to her, out there alone?'' or ''She shouldn't have gone into a neighborhood like that in the first place,'' have no place in any real understanding of why women are raped.

What Do We Know About Rape?

We know that rape is not ever the woman's fault, nor is it the result of psychological or physiological inadequacies on the part of the rapist. It is an act of violence. Rape represents a belief held by some men that they have the right to take any woman, at any time, simply because it makes them feel stronger, superior or tougher. Many feel rape is simply an unavoidable part of a culture such as ours which teaches that men are somehow better than women and therefore have the right to own and possess women as they see fit. One proof of this idea is that, as has been said, rape is not a universal crime. There are cultures, although few and far between, where rape is not even a part of the vocabulary for it simply never occurs. In our culture, however, rape is a common crime. Moreover, it appears to be increasing every year.

Rape Statistics

Rape is a crime that has not received enough attention in the past from criminologists, sociologists or psychologists. This is changing as more and more people are developing an increased knowledge about the crime of rape. We are starting to be able to study rape by looking at who is raped, when and where rape occurs and what kind of person rapes. Some typical patterns of rape are beginning to emerge from this study. However, these patterns do not explain all rapes. No two rapes are ever exactly alike. Therefore we have to be careful as we try to categorize rape. The patterns of rape are important only in that they provide us with additional information about who is likely to rape and be raped. This information may help us prevent some rapes.

Rape Victims

Most victims of rape tend to be young, under 25. Again, there are many exceptions to this rule. Young women, however, may be more likely victims than older women. Probably this is due to the fact that young women are more likely to be out alone, travel to and from work at irregular hours and be more trusting of men.

Minority women are also overrepresented in the rape statistics. However, this may be due to factors beyond being white, black or other minority. The income difference between minorities and non-minorities today means that minority women are more likely than white women to work outside the home and live in unsafe conditions. This may account for the higher likelihood of rape for minorities. We see, for example, that women of all races who must go and come from work at odd hours (such as nurses) have very high rape rates. Similarly, divorced women with low incomes have a higher incidence of rape than do divorced women with middle-class lifestyles, regardless of race. Social class and work patterns may explain, in part, the overrepresentation of minority women in rape statistics.

Where Rape Occurs

Rape occurs in the home very frequently; perhaps as many as one half of all rapes take place at home. Open areas and automobiles are also common areas for rape to occur. Again, these are patterns of rape rather than hard and fast rules. Rape has been cited as occurring anywhere from religious buildings to barroom floors.

Rapists

"Typical" rapists are difficult to describe. Some researchers have found patterns within the rapist population which indicate that a great many rapists are young. There is some indication that many rapists were themselves sexually abused as children. However, a great deal more research will be needed to determine the extent of such abuse among rapists. Many known rapists have histories of violent conduct, often with prior arrest records for rape and/or assault and battery. Most rapists operate alone. However, we can all remember reading about "gang rapes" participated in by college students, groups of friends or conventioning businessmen.

A word of caution about rape statistics needs to be introduced. Many of our attitudes about rape, based on statistics, are somewhat misleading. This is due to a number of very real problems in the study of rape. First, many victims of rape never report the crime to authorities. We have no way of knowing for certain how many women fail to report.

We also know that there is a difference between rapes that are reported and rapes that are not. In reported rapes, the rapist tends to be younger, poorer and unknown to the victim. Rapes committed by men who are known to the victim, although rarely reported, may account for well over one half of all rapes. (Acquaintance rape will be discussed in Chapter 7.)

Other factors which affect rape statistics include: the reluctance of victims to talk to researchers about their attacker; the tragic death of victims in the course of the rape; and the confusion of rape details in the minds of victims. Caution is advised in any reading of rape statistics. All of the statistics presented in this book will be carefully introduced for these reasons.

Until we can answer all of the questions about why rape occurs, we must continue in our attempts to learn more; to complete the jigsaw puzzle. We also need to make people aware of the known facts concerning the crime. Most importantly, we need to remember that rape is not the victim's fault. Only in these ways will we ever start to rid ourselves of this horrible crime.

3

Protecting Yourself
Against Rape

Nearly every book ever written about rape contains a section on how to prevent the crime. Often long and elaborate lists are presented explaining everything women should *not* do if they are to remain safe. Readers often put down such books with the feeling that they should never again venture out of their well-locked fortresses.

Prevention is a very controversial subject among women today. Some women seem to suggest that we must all stay inside, lock our doors and not come out until the crime of rape is eliminated. This author is very uneasy with such devastating suggestions. Should women be forced to do nothing and go nowhere simply because some men believe they have the right to be violent and cruel? The answer is a resounding "No!" Women should not have to pay for the crime of rape with both their bodies and their minds. Women should not be so intimidated by the crime that they forever "stay in their place."

We are left with a dilemma. The *reality* is that women are raped, and therefore fear it. The *wish* is that no woman should have to live differently because of the threat of rape. There is no easy solution to this dilemma, at least not at the present time. In this chapter, it is not suggested that the dilemma may be resolved with a few simplistic answers. Rape is a very real fear for all women. This is especially true for women who have been raped in the past. No one can tell you that your fears are silly or irrational. Conversely, no one should tell you to lock your doors and throw away the key.

One way to address this issue is to view the prevention of rape as similar to the prevention of other types of crime. We live in a time when crime seems to be everywhere. Beyond fearing rape, we worry about being burglarized, robbed and mugged. All of us, women and men alike, have to take some precautions against these crimes. There are no guarantees to ensure against being victimized. Even if we were to stay home twenty-four hours a day, we would still run certain risks. However, we can minimize those risks by following a few simple rules.

Another advantage gained from taking precautions is that if we feel safer, we lead happier, healthier lives. Often taking a few precautionary measures helps us to stop living in the constant shadow of our fears.

The following precautions are offered only as suggestions. Remember, you have the right to determine where you will go and when. However, these suggestions may help you avoid becoming the victim of any crime, including rape. The list given below is drawn from a variety of "do's and don'ts" lists and is by no means exhaustive or complete. Adopt and adapt these ideas as you see fit.

In Your Home

Many women are raped in the privacy of their homes. They may be raped by a trusted friend, an acquaintance or a complete stranger. Your home should be a haven, not a trap. To ensure your safety in your home, there are several precautions which you might consider:

- Make sure there are strong locks on your doors and windows.

- Avoid door locks which are complicated to open. (The longer you are outside your door, the greater your risks.)

- Make sure your entrance ways are well-lighted.

- If having a dog would make you feel safer and you are allowed to have one in your home or apartment, by all means adopt one.

- Do not let strangers into your home or apartment for any reason. Install a peephole in your door so that you may identify callers. If a stranger has run out of gas and wants to use your phone, place the call for him or her. If a repairperson has to come to your house, make arrangements in advance for a specific day and time so that when the person arrives you know this is indeed a repairperson. Always ask to see identification before you let a repairperson into your home. (Some women even ask the repairperson to wait outside while they call to verify the service call and the person's identity.)

- Do not trust anyone just because she or he looks nice. (Rapists can be anyone: police officers, men in three piece suits or the stereotypical "tough guy." They may even disguise themselves as women.)

- Do not list your first name on your mailbox or in the telephone book. (Some women who live alone put a fictitious man's name on their mailbox to indicate someone else is there.)

- Whether or not you live alone, rely on your neighbors if possible. Organize a neighborhood watch program if one does not exist in your area. Your local police will probably assist you in getting such a program started. One rather clever idea is to set up a signaling device with your neighbors. If you cannot get to the phone to call the police, you might at least be able to pull down a special shade or turn on a certain light. These pre-arranged signals let your neighbors know you need help.

- Keep phone numbers handy in case of an emergency.

- Call the police immediately if you suspect you are in danger.

Remember, too, that many rapes occur during the middle of the day. This is partly due to the fact that women often feel safer on a bright sunny afternoon and, as a result, take more chances. It does not hurt to follow the same precautions at noon that you would at midnight.

If You Are Out Alone

Some would-be attackers may use a variety of ploys or excuses in order to lure women into a dangerous situation. Being mentally prepared for these instances may help to prevent your being raped. Here are a few suggestions:

- If you are out walking alone and someone pulls up in a car to ask directions, do not approach the car. Stay on the sidewalk, keep walking and give directions from there. This way the person will have to control the car and talk to you at the same time. This makes it difficult for the driver to attempt anything else.

- If a man gets out of his car and approaches you, again try to keep moving. The further you are from him and his car, the more difficult it will be for him to drag you to it. Look for others on the street upon whom you might call to help give directions to the questioner. These suggestions also apply to the case where a man approaches you on foot. Keep walking and never lose sight of where he is and what he is doing.

While it may seem rude, your best choice of action may be to pretend that you cannot help him and suggest that he ask someone else. In any case, try to make a mental note of his appearance and manner of speech. If he is driving, the type of car, license plate number and direction of travel when he leaves should be noted. Even though this person may leave you alone, he may go on to assault someone else. Any information that you can provide to law enforcement officials may prove invaluable.

- A man may approach you claiming to be ill and ask that you take him home or to a hospital. Do not offer to drive him anywhere or invite him into your house. Suggest instead that you place a call for help on his behalf. Ask that he remain where he is while you go for help. In some cases, you may be able to ask a passer-by to join you in helping the person. If you do these things, and his ''illness'' is false, he will probably make some excuse and leave. If this happens, try to remember as much about him as possible and then call the police. This kind of prevention not only helps you, but helps others as well.

- A person may call to you for help from an alley or building. Do not approach him. Instead, keep a good distance away, ask him what the trouble is and then go elsewhere to call for help. Whether or not it turns out to be a real emergency, your best course of action is always to call the police, fire department or other emergency agency. You may wish to remain near the scene. However, let those who are trained for emergencies handle the situation. Of course, if the cry for help turns out to be a false alarm, your calling the authorities may result in the capture of a would-be rapist.

In Your Car

Many rapes occur as women are either approaching or leaving their automobiles. Sometimes a woman will be attacked while driving. These are particularly vulnerable times and merit special precautions:

- Always lock your car doors when you leave your car, and when you get back into it.

- As you approach your car from a distance, look around and under it. A common ploy is for rapists to hide under a car and then reach out to grab a woman's ankles when she reaches her car door.

- Have your key ready so you do not have to stand outside your car rummaging through your purse.

- Check the back seat before you enter your car.

- If you have car trouble, simply raise the hood and go back to your locked car. Wait for a patrol officer to offer you assistance. Under no circumstances should you hitchhike for help.

- If you are approached while parked or driving, keep your doors locked, sound the horn and step on the accelerator. A would-be rapist will probably run for cover.

- Try to park in well-lighted, populated parking areas. Many companies, schools and institutions now provide escort services to and from their employees' vehicles. Ask if this service is available to you.

Social Activities

The message of this chapter is to live your life fully, but still take some precautions. You will have to run some risks if you are to engage in social activities but the alternative is never to go anywhere. You may feel safer, however, if you keep the following in mind:

- If you are dating, try to learn something about a new date before you go out with him. If you have mutual friends, ask what they know about your new date.

- You may want to suggest that the first date or two be on your terms. Arrange to meet each other at a party or public area. Set up a double-date if at all possible. You will have to trust your instincts at some point, certainly, but taking time to get to know a person first may make you feel more comfortable.

- If you plan to go to a movie, party, night class or social engagement you may want to ask a friend to accompany you.

- If you are dropped off at home, ask the driver to wait until you are safely inside before leaving. Do the same for someone else if you are driving.

- If you travel alone to and from work every day, you may want to set up a car pool or at least a group of people who can walk to and from parking areas together.

- Try to avoid routine or predictable behavior. For instance, if every morning you leave your home at 10:00 a.m. to run errands, you may want to vary your schedule by leaving at a different time, traveling on a different route or shopping at different stores from time to time.

Weapons

Protecting yourself against rape by means of carrying a weapon is a subject upon which there is a great deal of disagreement. Some argue that your weapon might in fact be used against you if you are taken by surprise or momentarily frozen with fear. Others maintain carrying a weapon is a good deterrent to rape. As it stands now, no clear case can be made for either side of the argument. This is something only you can decide. If you choose to carry a weapon, be advised of these precautions:

- Make sure that you are in compliance with the laws in your area.

- Familiarize yourself fully with the use of the weapon so that it can be used effectively and not increase your vulnerability.

There are other ways to defend yourself which do not require the use of weapons:

- Sometimes the best protection is a loud, shrill whistle which may be carried with you at all times. Another noisemaker recently introduced is a small police siren. It is a compact device, about the size of a small flashlight. When activated, it emits a loud sound much like a police siren. The point is that no rapist wants to be caught. Anything you do to summon help may scare him off.

- In some states, you may buy mace or similar products to be sprayed into an attacker's face to blind him temporarily. Some women recommend carrying a can of aerosol spray paint. Not only might it startle the attacker to be sprayed in the face, a man covered with bright red paint might be more easily apprehended by the police. Again, there is always the risk that such items could be used against you, so handle them with care.

- A great many women today are enrolling in self-defense classes in order to protect themselves and not be overpowered by someone bigger and stronger. Classes in self-defense are offered around the country at low cost. A word of caution: Do not take for granted your newly-acquired skills. They may be meaningless against a handgun or a knife, so still be careful. Also, stay in practice so that you do not lose your skills. You may be no safer if, a year after your self-defense class, you can no longer do what you were taught.

If You Are Attacked

Women often ask what they can do if they are approached and threatened with rape. It would be wonderful if there were one absolutely foolproof rule to be followed in all such cases. Unfortunately, this is not so. It is important that you think about what you *might* do in such a situation. However, each rape is different and no plan will work every time.

We have all heard of women who prevented rape by taking some measure that worked in a particular situation. One woman laughs in the rapist's face and he leaves her alone. Another acts as if she wants to be raped, and thus disappoints the rapist. Still another woman struggles until she gets away. Some women "talk" their way out of rape by claiming to have herpes or some dreaded disease. Women have even vomited or urinated on their would-be rapists, thereby scaring them away.

It is easy to read about such cases and perhaps decide upon a specific course of action should the need arise. Remember, each rapist and each rape situation is different. Some rapists *want* you to fight back because it makes them all the more determined to rape you. Other rapists are frightened by the struggle and run away. Some rapists want you to "enjoy" it. Other rapists are uninterested in a women who pretends not to be repelled by their attacks. It is certainly wise to think about how you would react to rape. However, until you are faced with the immediate danger you cannot plan your defense in detail. Regardless, the time spent in initial planning is not wasted and will probably help you to remain calm in the event you are attacked.

One rule to keep in mind if attacked is to try to talk to the would-be rapist. Conversation may give you the time you need to think of an escape. It might also give you the insight you need to get away from him. His weakness may become evident by what he says, and you can use that weakness to your advantage. Such tactics may also increase the chances of someone else arriving on the scene to help you. If nothing else, the comments your attacker makes to you may later provide valuable information for law enforcement officials in their efforts to apprehend him.

The most important thing for you to remember is that planning for what you might do and say if attacked is not a guarantee against being raped. Even if you come up with what seems to be a good tactic, it may be the very behavior which makes the rapist that much more violent. That is not your fault. You may even be temporarily frozen and unable to behave in any way. That is a typical response to danger and also not your fault. *Do what you must do in order to survive.* Do not blame yourself later for what you might view, with hindsight, as a "mistake."

Even if you are attacked, despite your precautions, or if you are not successful in getting away, despite your protective measures—you can recover from being raped. Your recovery will be easier if you are prepared. Have the phone numbers for the police, a hospital and your rape crisis center handy. You can use the space provided at the back of this book to record such information.

4

Your Response to Rape

The one thing that matters most if you are raped is how you think and feel about yourself. How *you* feel is more important than how any one else feels. This includes the police, judges, your family, friends or acquaintances. How you think and feel will determine your health and ability to function and find satisfaction. Your thoughts and feelings will be important in the short run, as well as for the future. Remember that there are no ''typical'' responses to rape. No two people react to the violence itself, nor recover from it, in exactly the same manner. Whatever you feel, whether or not it is similar to what researchers have found for other victims, it is an acceptable part of your adjustment.

There may be, however, many similarities between you and other victims of rape. Knowing that you are not alone is important. Keep this in mind as we examine the ways in which many women respond both emotionally and physically during and after the rape.

To a great extent fear determines what you do during a rape. Whether or not you are aware of it at the time, you are making a judgment of a threatening situation and responding according to the basic law of survival common to all living things. Soldiers on the battlefield may fight bravely or duck for cover, depending on the danger level of the moment. Their brains process the threat and direct their actions accordingly. The fact that well-trained soldiers are more likely to perform well in combat is testimony to the value of preparedness. However, even well-trained soldiers, or people trained in self-defense, may not act in the ways which they were taught when faced with a real or unexpected threat. The point is that while preparedness may help you avoid being raped, it may also be ineffective. There is no reward in feeling guilty or blaming yourself for how you acted during the rape. If you have been raped, the fact that you can read this book now says something very important. *You survived, therefore, you did the right thing.* You must realize that you did what you did in order to stay alive.

How Some Women Respond To Rape

There are many possible responses to rape. For that reason you should not look back on what you did or felt as a way to judge yourself. What we are talking about is fear and violence. Therefore, any response is possible. Some women talk to their attackers during the rape, promising anything, bargaining for freedom or just trying to make the attacker believe that his victim is a nice person who should be allowed to live. Sometimes when an individual is faced with something terrible, the brain simply withdraws from reality. As a result, many women freeze or their minds focus on a past experience that was not horrible. Some women fight. Others attempt to flee. Some focus on their attacker, cataloging every detail that might be helpful to the police. Quite naturally, many women are physically sickened by rape and respond by vomiting, urinating or defecating either during or after the attack. As you can see, almost any response is possible during a rape.

During the course of a rape, some victims respond physically (for example, with orgasm or lubrication) as if they were love-making. Rape is not love-making, yet the body may respond in similar ways. Orgasm is a physical response to physical stimula-tion. Likewise, lubrication is your body's method of protecting the sensitive genital area. Do not confuse these physical responses with sexual desire or pleasure. This is simply your body's way of protecting itself.

Remember you need not feel guilty for how you responded, physically or emotionally, during the attack. Do not blame yourself for wanting to survive. In looking back on the attack, keep in mind the following points:

- Do not evaluate your behavior by falsehoods that other people may impose upon you, or by myths you were taught prior to the rape. People who say to you, "I would have fought to the death to preserve my honor," or "I'd just relax and enjoy the inevitable," have obviously never been raped. Hindsight is of little value, and hindsight that results in guilt and self-blame has no value at all.

- Remember that most rapists would have raped someone else had you not been there. They are not interested in sexual gratification with a particular woman. Rather, the real reason for the attack is the rapist's need to intimidate and abuse women in general. The rape occurred because of the rapist's deficiencies. You did not cause the rape.

- You should not blame yourself for where you were, or for what you may have said. You are not responsible for the behavior of a rapist.

- Guilt is almost a universal feeling among rape victims. This usually occurs because victims focus on the sexual aspect of rape rather than the violence. No matter what you did, there is no cause for guilt. No one ever blames people robbed at gunpoint for giving up their money.

- Do not blame yourself for judgments you may have made before or during the attack. If the rapist was a trusted person such as a doctor or police officer, disguised as such, or even disguised as another woman, do not blame yourself for being deceived. There is no way to tell what a rapist may look like, so there is no point in assuming that had you been more careful you would have spotted him in time to escape.

• Unfortunately, it is all too common for women to be raped by someone they know, trust or even love. Remember, the victim is not to blame for the violent actions of another, even if he is a friend or lover. (This type of situation will be discussed in Chapter 7.)

Recovery

Your long-term response to having been raped may follow no set pattern or time schedule. Some women find that they recover quickly, others feel they will never get over the trauma. It may seem difficult to believe at first, but you will eventually learn to cope with having been raped. You will recover in your own way and at your own pace. As was mentioned earlier, there is no model for recovery but the description which follows includes some things you might experience as you do recover.[1]

The First Stage

From the first twenty-four hours to about a week or so after the attack, you may experience a feeling of acute distress and severe anxiety. In other words, you are very upset. This is the first after-shock of your attack and is considered by many researchers to be the first stage of your recovery. Not really believing what has happened to you or denying that the rape ever occurred is also

---

[1]See the work of Ann Wolbert Burgess and Lynda Lytle Holmstrom for more information on Rape Trauma Syndrome. Different authors discuss the stages of rape recovery in a variety of way. What is presented here is a brief summary of some common stages of rape recovery.

common. Other women have reported a sudden need to turn to others for guidance as they come to question their own capabilities.

You may encounter emotional and/or physical problems such as recurrent headaches or nightmares, nausea, confusion, paralysis, sleeplessness, loss of appetite and the like. Some women experience what might best be called an emotional void; they find it difficult to feel anything for awhile. Dwelling on the rape itself and feeling "dirty" because of it, or being fearful that it will happen again, are also feelings which may occur during this time. You might also find yourself spending a lot of time worrying about hospital bills, finding a new apartment, getting time off work or resuming your sex life. All of these thoughts and emotions may come and go suddenly and without warning. Do not think of yourself as irrational or "going crazy." Such responses are very normal. This phase will pass, and soon you will be able to start to make sense of your feelings.

There are some practical steps which you can take to make this time a bit easier to bear:

- Remember that you are most important. Whatever others may say or feel, your primary concern should be yourself. If you are a wife and mother this may be more difficult. However, still try to have those around you, who care about you, give you the time you need to start to rebuild your life.

- Attend to the physical side effects of the rape. Some of the physical symptoms mentioned above may be due to medications you have been given as treatment for the rape. Check with your doctor to see if a change in medication is advisable. Also, if after receiving treatment at the hospital you still feel bad physically, see your doctor. Do not assume that a persistent headache, stomachache, or dizziness are all anxiety related. Find out for sure. You may have an injury that was overlooked during the initial treatment.

- As soon as possible, try to resume your regular routine. This will help you overcome the initial effects of your trauma and help you to organize your thoughts. It will also help to convince yourself that life can, and will continue.

- Make some decisions. There will be many to make: medical, legal, those concerning your children, what to do if you have become pregnant due to the rape and so forth. You have just come through an experience where control has been taken from you by a man needing to dominate women. Regain that control, and your self respect, by making at least a few decisions. It is always a good idea to listen to others; for awhile you may even want them to run your life to some extent. However, the sooner you start running your own life, the sooner you will recover. Decision making is an essential part of this process.

The Second Stage

Typically, the next stage in the recovery process begins the first few weeks after the rape. This is really an extension of the initial reaction described above. During this time, you may feel calmer overall but there is still an underlying distress. You may feel more defensive, both emotionally and physically, or you may see yourself as somewhat helpless or confused. You may experience sudden mood swings, or become suddenly angered by things that would not have bothered you prior to the rape.

What you may find even more troublesome during this time is that you may not be able to feel anger toward the rapist, especially if you often become angry at family or friends for "little things." *This does not mean that you secretly enjoyed the rape.* There are many theories which explain why some women initially have difficulty feeling anger toward their rapist. It may be that the lack of anger is a survival reaction on your part. Subconsciously you might believe that if you are not angry at the rapist, he will have no reason to attack you again. Others feel that the problem is more straight-forward. Rape usually results in a great deal of self-blame and self-punishment. As such, it is hard to be angry at the rapist when you are blaming and punishing yourself.

Giving up control over their lives to others is a response some women display during this time. This may include a sort of self-imposed isolation. This behavior may be both good and bad depending upon who you are, and who is stepping in for you. For instance, the loss of privacy and independence that comes with turning control over to someone else may give you a perspective from which to judge what you will want and need at some point in the future. It may also give you some time to reorder your thoughts and priorities. Unfortunately, depending on others for too long can have its drawbacks. It may make it difficult to resume your normal life and to be in charge of your own thoughts, feelings and behaviors. There are several important points you should keep in mind during this time:

- The erratic behavior you may experience during this time does not mean that you have become neurotic or crazy. It is just part of the normal recovery process. Your mind is trying to make sense out of what has happened.

- Many of the suggestions that were given during the first recovery stage apply here also. The most important recommendation is that you should work to regain control of your life as soon as possible.

The Third Stage

A few weeks after the rape, you may start to feel fine. You find that you go through your day without having thought of the rape very much. To yourself and to others, you seem completely recovered. This is called *apparent readjustment* and may last a few weeks to a few months. During this time your mind is processing, or making sense of, the events of the rape, how you feel about others and how you feel about yourself. This is a protective mechanism that lets you have a somewhat normal lifestyle while the subconscious does the difficult work of trying to straighten out feelings and memories. This is the time when you really want to reestablish your previous lifestyle as much as possible. This is also an important time for you to keep in communication with those you have found to be most supportive. Let them know you still want and need them, as they may find it easy to forget the rape if they think you are totally recovered.

The Final Stage

Just when you think you have put the entire rape experience behind you, many of the old problems you first encountered reappear. Depression, anxiety, fear, insomnia, headaches, unpredictable moods, mistrust of men, feelings of guilt and sexual disturbances may unexpectedly manifest themselves. This stage may be called *reorganization/integration* and may not begin until several weeks or months after the rape. These feelings are nothing but the same problems you encountered initially. They have been buried in your mind, waiting to reappear when you are better able to cope with them. Now you will start to find solid, permanent solutions to these problems based on the better judgment and frame of mind that the passing weeks have allowed you to establish.

It may also be that this is the first time you realize any real anger toward the rapist. This is a healthy reaction. It will finally allow you the needed opportunity to vent this emotion. It also indicates that you are blaming yourself less and the rapist more. This is as it should be. Coincidently, this will probably also be the time when, if the rapist is caught and prosecuted, the trial will be underway. Having started to put the blame on the rapist will help you better deal with the court proceedings and, conversely, the public prosecution of the rapist will help you relieve your unwarranted feelings of guilt.

You may decide during this time that some change in lifestyle is in order. Such decisions usually result from a need to feel safe and secure. No one can argue with this. However, try to avoid extremes. Do not become a hermit, stop taking night classes or going to parties. Try to choose simple, rational ways of improving your safety. Getting a large dog or improving door and window locks are good steps to take. You may want to travel alone less and more in the company of friends. Whatever you choose, try not to make yourself a prisoner of your fears. Your recovery will not be complete until you can begin to enjoy those activities which were important to you before you were raped.

What Research Shows

Research indicates that at some point, maybe a year or so after the rape, you will have recovered. Yet, even after the problems mentioned above have faded away, you may still carry some aspects of the rape with you. These may be positive in that you now see yourself as a new and stronger person. Or, they may be negative because of lingering guilt, lowered self-esteem or fear. If negative feelings do persist, try not to take this as a sign that you will never again lead a satisfying, happy or ''normal'' life. Most women do overcome these negative feelings and, in time, you will too.

What has been described above is really only an outline of what you may experience during your recovery from rape. Exactly how you recover will depend upon what you experienced, how you responded to it and what kinds of steps were taken by you and others during the recovery period. How any one woman recovers is dependent upon many factors, a few of which are listed below:

- *Medical help.* Women who seek immediate medical attention after rape tend to recover faster emotionally due to the support that society provides for those who have been physically injured. Having a doctor or nurse attend to your wounds may also help to make it clear in your mind that you have been seriously wronged, and that it is not your fault.

- *Reporting the crime.* Whether or not you decide to try to prosecute, reporting the rape may help to convince you that a crime against you, and not by you, has occurred. This may make your emotional recovery easier.

- *Feeling responsible.* Being friendly to the rapist before you knew of his intentions, hitchhiking, wearing certain clothing or making what you later consider to be an error in judgment, may result in your feeling responsible for the rape. The more responsible you feel, the longer it will take for you to recover. One of the main ideas throughout this book is that *you are not responsible for the behavior of a rapist.* Try to bear this in mind as you cope with your feelings.

- *Divorced women.* If you are divorced or separated, it may be more difficult for you to recover emotionally from rape. Any guilt or self-blame for the divorce is often compounded by the guilt that results from the rape. You may also be more keenly aware of the impact of the rape upon your children, fearing for their safety and emotional well-being.

- *Age.* If you are an older woman, especially an older woman living alone, you may wonder if in fact you did not secretly wish to be raped out of loneliness or sexual desire. You may come to question your behavior, assuming a burden of guilt for the rape. Research has found that many older women share these feelings and that it is normal for you to try to look to yourself for blame. Remember that a rapist does not know or care about your feelings. Therefore, despite your age, marital status, sexual desires or feelings of loneliness, *you did not cause your rape.*

Recovering from rape is very much like recovering from the death of a loved one. The victim feels a loss and goes through a period of mourning. If you are raped, you will have to face this and you will have to find your own way of recovering. However, finding your own way does not mean that you must do it alone. Feel free to talk to people who are important to you. Share your feelings, fears, strengths and perceived weaknesses. Rely on your local rape crisis center and the multitude of support services it offers. Attitudes are changing. One benefit of that change is that many people are more knowledgeable about rape, more supportive of those who have been raped and more open to their needs. *Remember, you can recover.*

5

Family, Friends and Others

There was a time when the victims of rape were forced to endure their suffering in silence. Rape was a "closet" crime, not to be discussed openly. Women feared that if they tried to talk about what happened to them they would be blamed and ridiculed.

Fortunately, this situation is slowly changing. Today more than ever, support for rape victims is available. Victims no longer need to hide the crime committed against them, ashamed of what others might think. Increasingly, people are willing to help rape victims, not hurt them further. *You should not have to suffer alone the pain and frustrations caused by rape.*

The support now offered to rape victims is a major advancement over earlier times. Research has shown that rape victims recover more quickly if they have others in their social worlds to whom they may turn. If you are raped, sharing your experience with those around you who care about you, and will listen to you, will be tremendously therapeutic. If you are raped, you will face a very vulnerable period of time in your life. You may feel frightened and upset. You will need the support and love of other people to let you know that you can recover.

This chapter will help you find and use support from others. Special attention is paid to your family members, friends, co-workers and volunteer or professional counselors. Another obvious source of support may be available from your husband or close partner. This special kind of relationship will be explored in greater depth in the next chapter.

Two points need to be made about the interaction between rape victims and people who are an important part of their lives. First, despite the vast improvements in the way rape victims are seen by others, certain problems may still arise during the process of confronting the trauma of rape with another person. You should be aware of these "pitfalls," and know how to cope with them. This will protect you from being hurt. Second, there is a chance that a member of your family or someone else whom you love will someday be a victim of rape. If you are ever in the position of being asked for support by a rape victim, this information will be helpful.

Your Family

One of the most obvious sources of support for you may exist among the people to whom you would turn with any other problem; the members of your family. Parents, sisters and brothers or other relatives are quite often the people who offer the most support to rape victims. It may seem surprising, but often the act of merely talking to someone in your family can be of tremendous help. If you are raped, many advantages are gained from talking to your family. After all, it is quite likely that your family cares every bit as much as you do about your recovery.

Feel free to turn to the members of your family to whom you feel most close with your fears, concerns and problems. This may involve sitting down for a good long talk. Maybe you will want to express your anger toward the rapist to a sympathetic ear; a sounding board. Often, it is the secondary problems that most need discussing; the reaction of your spouse to the rape, what your boss said about it at work, bills that need paying. The important thing to remember is that if you want to talk about how you feel, do so with someone in your family whom you trust. You may be surprised to find how much it helps.

Another benefit of turning to members of your family for support is that quite often they can point out what you might be missing simply because you are upset. For example, they may be able to suggest positive steps which you could take on the road to recovery. These might include developing new activities, taking precautions to feel safer or working toward prosecuting your attacker.

The period directly following the crime of rape is a very traumatic one. If you have family members who want to listen, make you feel better and support your cause, do not hesitate to turn to them as much as necessary. It is one of the most important aspects of rape recovery.

As was mentioned, however, turning to your family after you are raped may result in some less than desirable effects as well. It is important that you are aware of these problems so that you know how to recognize and avoid them. Most of the problems stem from the fact that, because your family loves you, they may try to do too much to help. Moreover, again because your family cares, they will have their own emotional reactions to your rape. These reactions may not always be in your best interest. Your family may feel anger, guilt, frustration and fear, much in the same way that you do. Their own reactions may limit their ability to be there for you when you need them. A few of the negative family responses which you might face are described below:

- Your family may react with anger, "I'm going to kill the guy who did this to you!" Although your family certainly has the right to be angry, such expressions do little to make you feel better. In fact, they may even worsen your emotional state. Their anger may add to your list of worries. The new possibility that someone you love will be hurt or arrested while trying to seek revenge may increase your burden. You may feel responsible in some way for the apparent trouble you have caused your family.

- Your family may respond by wanting to take charge of your life. Suddenly you may be confronted with orders to quit your job, move home, change your neighborhood or stay home every night. You may feel that you are being watched around the clock, as if you are a little girl again. Quite probably this reaction on the part of your family stems from two sources: their need to protect you from further attacks, and their sense of guilt for allowing this to happen to you in the first place. Even though you know they are not at fault, their guilt feelings are real to them.

- Your family may over-react and treat you as if you are an invalid, in need of immediate and complete psychological care. Quite often families arrange for a victim to see religious leaders, psychiatrists, counselors and family physicians. Your family members may feel that they have suddenly been thrust into a totally unknown area and see "experts" as the only solution. You, on the other hand, may feel no need or desire whatsoever to talk to these professionals.

- Members of your family may seem to deny the reality of the rape. They may go out of their way to avoid the subject, keep conversation light and cheery and speak in hushed tones whenever certain topics come up. They may be very secretive about the rape, not wanting the neighbors, cousins and grandparents to know. All of this may serve to make you feel more traumatized, as if your rape is something too horrible for words.

Are there solutions to these potential family problems? Quite often the answer is yes. However, there are no perfect formulas which you might follow. In general, the key is always to talk, as openly as possible, about how all of you feel. Encourage your family to discuss their emotions, if they are not too upsetting to you. More importantly, encourage your family to listen to you. Remind them of your strengths lest they forget your capabilities. Suggest that your family does some reading on the subject of rape, or even talk to an expert themselves. As they come to understand their own reactions to your attack, they will be better able to serve your needs. You may want to seek out the family members who are most supportive and ask that they explain to the rest of the family what it is you need to hear, and how you need to be treated.

Talking to your family can be an important part of your recovery. But you have the right not to be hampered by their negative responses. You have the right to decide what to say, when to say it and to whom. Hopefully, in time, all members of your family will come to understand this and help in the ways which are most beneficial to you.

Friends

In some ways, talking to a friend about your rape has certain advantages over talking to your family. You may choose to restrict your conversations to friends, especially if you find your family to be less than helpful. The choice is certainly yours.

A trusted friend, or set of friends, can perform all of the functions which the family can. They can listen, point out your strengths, offer support. Moreover, they may be able to do so more objectively. Although they care about you, they may feel less responsible and emotionally-charged than your family. Also, your friends may know you in ways that your family does not. You may have an easier time talking to friends regarding your concerns about sexuality, for example. Finally, your friends are your friends because they care about you and share your interests. You may turn to them with your problems, or simply for a diversion. Sometimes it helps to know that you have someone to call, night and day.

If at all possible, try to share your emotions after the rape with friends of both sexes. Women and men may assume very different roles in response to rape. Each role may provide you with comfort. Research has shown that a female friend is of most help as a confidant and "soul-mate." Other women have themselves feared rape and know something about what you are experiencing. Men, on the other hand, may be able to provide you with something entirely different. Having been demoralized and degraded by one man (the rapist), you may want to know that another man appreciates you as a worthwhile and capable person—not as just a piece of "property." Perhaps such male/female differences should not exist as stereotypes. Certainly there are exceptions to each rule. However, many rape victims find these differences to be true.

The friends to whom you turn after you have been raped should always be people who help you, not hurt you. Avoid interaction with friends who are judgmental in any way. Remember, you did not cause your rape and you certainly do not need to hear any accusations to that effect. It simply is not true, despite what some so-called friends might imply.

You might also want to seek out friends who offer you the opportunity to set your own pace. Do not be forced by well-meaning friends to do or say anything that makes you feel uncomfortable. Trust your own judgment. You will know when it is time to talk about the rape, focus on other matters or just relax.

Work

Choosing to tell co-workers about your rape will depend on the type of relationship you have with them. Your friends at work might offer you tremendous support and guidance. If you have to lose time from the job, or if your performance is reduced temporarily, they may be more understanding if they know the reason. You do not have to feel ashamed of what has happened.

Some rape victims report however, that they are treated differently at work once it is known that they were raped. This is not only unfair, it is illegal. If you think you are being treated poorly at work, talk to your supervisor, file a grievance, turn to your rape crisis center for support or seek legal counsel. *No one has the right to penalize you in any way for being raped.*

Rape Crisis Centers

One of the greatest advances of our time with regards to rape is the opening of literally hundreds of rape crisis centers across the country. These centers mean that many rape victims now have someone to seek out for help, information and support. Most centers are operated by volunteers, women and men who are concerned about the crime of rape and want to become involved in its elimination. They usually have both training and experience in dealing with rape victims. The volunteers (called "advocates" in many cases) offer twenty-four hour a day support for rape victims. They inform victims of their rights, teach about area laws and procedures and provide counseling services. Some conduct community education programs, arrange child care or temporary shelter, supply financial support to victims and so forth. Many regions are now served by rape crisis centers. Their presence has meant that a great many victims have been able to obtain medical, legal and emotional support from trained para-professionals.

One important job of the rape crisis advocate is to help rape victims seek out and obtain the very best medical and legal support following an attack. If you are raped, you will probably want to contact your local rape crisis center for these services (see Chapters 8-10). Another critical job of the rape crisis advocate, however, is to help meet your emotional needs following the rape. Your advocate may counsel you or arrange for counseling through the rape crisis center. Either way, you will be put in touch with someone who has helped other rape victims to recover.

A rape advocate is often the ideal person to talk to about your rape. The rape advocate knows, perhaps better than anyone, the kinds of feelings you are experiencing. Moreover, the advocate knows what you need to hear following the crime of rape. Another advantage of turning to a rape advocate is that he or she is in a position of being detached from your everyday life. There is less likelihood, therefore, of the rape advocate feeling guilty or responsible for your rape as might your friends or family. This means that the advocate has the ability to look at your situation objectively, encourage you to be practical and help you identify your strengths as well as correct your weaknesses. The trained advocate knows that you will recover from your rape, at your own pace. The advocate also knows that sometimes a good listener can make a tremendous contribution to your recovery.

If you do not know how to go about finding a rape crisis center in your area, refer to Appendix A for some suggestions. Whether or not you have been raped, write down the phone number of your nearest rape crisis center in the "Be Prepared" section of this book (Appendix B) and keep it handy. If you are raped, you may want to call the center immediately. Your advocate will meet you at the hospital, police station or your home. From that moment on you will have a friend at your side to provide you with invaluable information and support.

Professional Counselors

There was a time when many professional counselors had no interest in rape victims. This was due, in part, to a belief that victims were at fault for their attack. Fortunately, this is no longer the case. Many professional counselors now open their doors to the victims of rape. Often their services are provided free of charge through rape crisis centers or community mental health organizations. Whether you choose a psychiatrist, psychologist or counselor, you may find individual counseling beneficial as you work through your reaction to rape. You may even choose to seek out counseling for yourself and other members of your family, including your spouse or children. You do not necessarily require professional counseling if you are raped, but you may choose it if you think it might be helpful.

If you do see a counselor, the process you might expect will vary greatly from one professional to another. There are many different kinds of treatment plans, and each professional chooses the plan that she or he thinks is best. There is a very good chance, however, that talking to your counselor will be quite similar to talking to a friend. You need not worry about fearing the unexpected when you first enter the counselor's office. You will be asked to talk about your feelings concerning the rape, and about how you have been coping since the attack. You will come to see that you have done many things correctly since the rape and that you are not the "failure" you might have thought. You will explore additional coping mechanisms that might be used to solve the problems you face. You may learn more about how to deal with family and friends who are making your recovery difficult. The counselor may even talk to those friends and family members on your behalf.

One note of caution should be introduced in any discussion of professional counseling services. Remember that counselors are people with their own values, beliefs and attitudes. Most counselors are extremely helpful to rape victims. If you should feel, however, that the counselor with whom you discuss your problem is less than totally accepting and supportive, by all means discontinue such services. You do not deserve to be degraded by any other person, and this includes a professional counselor. Just because a counselor has had specialized training does not give him or her the right to question what you did or did not do during or after your attack. Simply stop your counseling visits or choose another professional. You may want to consider reporting the inappropriate behavior of the counselor to her or his superior.

It cannot be stressed enough that any decision to see a professional counselor is yours and yours alone. If you are raped, you certainly do not become "sick" overnight and in need of special care. Many rape victims recover from the crime without ever talking to a professional. The counselor is there only if *you* feel he or she might be helpful.

In Conclusion

Turning to other people for help and support after you are raped is a very positive step on the road to recovery. Do not hesitate to seek out such support, always bearing in mind the following:

- If you are raped, you need to talk about it. Locking up all of your emotions without any release will not help you to recover. Certainly you will still need your quiet, private time. But, you should also find people who are willing to listen to your concerns.

- If you are raped, you need support, not criticism. Some people may try to blame you, criticize your actions or in some way make you feel worse. Because you may be vulnerable to others' opinions of you, avoid these encounters whenever possible. Expect others to respect you for who you are. If they are invasive, tell them you are not in the mood to talk, or even suggest that they discuss their feelings with someone else. Always remind yourself of what you are doing right, rather than those behaviors of which others might disapprove.

- If you are raped, you are in charge. This is the most important point to be made regarding the people in your life. Your feelings are most important. You have the privilege of deciding what should be said, to whom and when. You also have the privilege of deciding what advice to accept, and what to reject. You need not be forced to act in any particular way even though you are being pressured by well-meaning friends, relatives or so-called experts. You may find it helpful to seek out those persons who understand this, and use them as buffers between yourself and those who seem insensitive to your needs.

If you are raped, you can recover. No matter how you are treated by others, you can still direct your own life. You did it before you were raped, and you will do it again. Sometimes other people may slow down this process. It is more likely, however, that they will help with your recovery. Feel free to rely upon helpful others but *know that your own personal resources will provide an important foundation for your recovery.*

6

Husbands, Lovers
and Children

One very special issue surrounding the crime of rape is its effect on the victim's relationship with her husband, boyfriend, fiance, roommate or lover. (The word "partner" will be used throughout this chapter to refer to any person who fits into these roles.) Some rape victims find it difficult to resume normal relations with this important person in their lives. What is especially troublesome is that this person is often the very individual with whom the victim has shared other problems and emotions in the past.

Rape is an assault on relationships, and often entire families. If you are raped, you may find that you are doubly attacked. Not only have you been assaulted, but your relationship with your family also changes. Sometimes the nature of the emotional bond between you and your partner becomes altered and quite often the sexual relationship changes. You may also find that your relationship with your children is different as a result of the rape. The primary reason for these unfortunate changes is that when you are raped, the people around you feel victimized too. They have their own emotional reactions, fears and problems. If these reactions are out of sync with yours, communication becomes difficult. When communication deteriorates, you, and those who live under the same roof with you, feel alone and isolated.

No one can minimize these problems. If you have been raped, you already know just how strained family relations can become as a result. This chapter describes the kind of reactions you might expect from others, why you see the reactions you do and how to respond to such reactions. This information may help you not only to deal with the reactions of those close to you, but also may maximize *their* ability to make a significant contribution to your recovery. First, your relationship with your partner will be examined. A word about your relationship with your children will follow.

The Emotional Relationship

The major problem a rape victim faces as she tries to resume normal interaction with her partner is that she and her partner are two unique people who each view the rape very differently. "He doesn't understand me," and "I just don't know what she wants," are two commonly heard expressions in the interactions occurring between victims and their partners. Each person does, in fact, have very different feelings about the rape. These differences may make it difficult for them to communicate with each other on the same level. It is as if two people who have been very intimate now suddenly seem to come from two separate worlds.

New Feelings Toward Your Partner

We have already seen some of the ways that you, the victim, might feel. Guilt, anxiety, self-blame, depression and irritability are but a few of the common emotional responses to the crime of rape. Two additional feelings may emerge which have not yet been fully discussed. First, some rape victims find that they grow more and more dependent on their partner for protection. If you are raped, you might suddenly be afraid to leave your partner's side. You cling to a man to be protected from other men. Ironically, this dependency can lead to feelings of resentment as well. You may resent a life which revolves around men whom you may see as both protective and as the people from whom you need protection.

A second reaction you may feel could very well be an out-growth of the first. You may suddenly be angry at *all* men, including your own partner. Now the "little things" that you may have done for your partner unquestioningly in the past (such as fix his meals or pick up after him) may seem monumental and unacceptable.

Your Partner's Reactions

These two, perhaps new, feelings toward your partner are discussed because they have a direct bearing on your relationship. Can they be resolved to your, and his, satisfaction? Before we try to answer that question, let's talk about his emotional reaction to your rape.

If you are raped, one thing your partner may feel is anger. He is angry at the rapist and wants to see him pay for what he has done. But he may also be angry at you. Whether he admits it to himself or not, he may be plagued by nagging doubts about what you might have done to "entice" the rapist. He may be angry at you for being careless or not fighting hard enough to repel the rapist's attacks. He may feel that his "property" has been violated and that he needs someone to blame.

He may also feel isolated from you in a way he cannot control. Even though he wants to help and support you, he feels clumsy and awkward; afraid he will do or say something to make you feel worse. He may even feel guilty because you are going through something caused by a man, and he suffers guilt simply by association. As a result, he feels he has no right to intrude upon your pain, possibly making it even more unbearable.

It is quite likely that he will feel confused by your statements and actions, much as you are confused by his. The two of you have little basis for comparison to evaluate how the other feels. You are both emotionally caught in the throes of the rape and it becomes difficult to stand back and objectively put yourselves in each other's shoes. You have both been affected by the crime of rape, directly and indirectly. You have to recover, not only as a couple, but as two individuals, each with private feelings.

Finding Resolution

The angers and resentments you feel toward each other need to be confronted if they are to be resolved. Left unspoken, they could fester and create serious problems at some later time. The first step toward resolution, therefore, is communication. To whatever extent possible, talk about how you feel toward each other, and about yourselves individually. Tell each other openly and honestly what you both should or should not do to help ease the adjustment.

Certainly each of you may experience real, but often quite different, emotional responses to the rape. These differences in response may seem to set up artificial walls between you. It is important that you talk about your responses with each other in order to establish "common ground." Where do you agree about what has happened? Knowing that common ground exists may give you the added courage necessary to face those areas where you disagree. Identify and outline your differences. Try to work on them one by one. The more dialogue that occurs between you and your partner, the more you will feel as if you are sharing the trauma rather than living in two separate worlds.

Some couples find that turning to an objective outsider improves communication. A trusted friend, parent, advocate or professional counselor may be able to help you to understand each other better, and to work more closely together during your recovery. The outsider may serve to bring together two emotional positions which seem quite far apart. Any kind of outside support which encourages you to talk about your feelings will help to diffuse pent-up emotions which may slow your recovery and harm your relationship. Do not hesitate to seek such assistance if you think it might be helpful.

Even in the closest and most open of relationships, two people may find that they still disagree on an appropriate response to rape. If your partner's viewpoint is making your own recovery impossible, you may want to avoid the subject temporarily with each other. Talk to other people who will be more helpful as you work through your emotions, and have your partner do the same. You need not cope with any additional problems your partner may be causing; the rape itself is challenging enough. If he makes you feel worse with his anger and blame, suggest that he talk to someone else about his emotions. A companion volume to this book, *If She Is Raped: A Book for Husbands, Fathers and Male Friends* by Alan McEvoy and Jeff Brookings, will be quite helpful for your partner. You may find, in time, that you and your partner are able to come back together and discuss the rape more rationally than before. Give each other this private time when you find you absolutely cannot communicate.

Some rape victims report that their relationship not only survives the trauma of rape, but emerges a deeper and more meaningful one. Couples discover that they feel closer to one another than before. Other couples, however, never learn to adjust to the rape and some end their relationship as a result. The future of your relationship will depend on two things: how you each recover from the rape separately and how you communicate about the rape together. You may have to shift your attention from yourself to your partner and back again. Taking care of yourself *and* each other is a demanding and important task.

The Sexual Relationship

If you are raped, resuming and maintaining sexual relations with your partner may seem difficult. This is not unusual. One, or both of you, may feel uneasy in sexual relations. It is important to remember that the sex you shared with your partner before the rape is as separate from the rape itself as any other aspect of your behavior. Rape is an act of violence, not sexual closeness. Because you and your partner may view sexuality differently as a result of the rape, sexual relations can become a problem.

If you have been raped, your sense of sexuality may be dramatically changed. You may enter a phase of celibacy, wanting nothing at all to do with sex. You may mistakenly confuse sex with rape, and try to avoid it altogether.

On the other hand, you may follow another quite different pattern, that of wanting sex more than ever. Some speculate that this common reaction provides a mechanism for you to prove to yourself that sex is still good, moral and acceptable, despite what happened during the rape.

Changes of any type in your sexual behavior are normal responses to the crime of rape. You may question your own sexuality. You may even wonder if you really wanted to be raped. You may feel that your morality is on the line, a situation which can hardly help but affect your sexuality. Remember, *the fact that you were raped has nothing to do with your sexuality.*

Another, more straight-forward problem you may face is that the act of sex itself is reminiscent of the rape. Let's look at a simple, but appropriate, example. If you have ever been in a car accident, you probably know that every time you drive by the same location, maybe even years later, you remember the incident. Trauma is stored in memory and triggered by familiar connections.

Even though rape is not really an act of sexual intimacy, you may find that you "flashback" to your attack each time your partner lovingly does the same sexual thing which the rapist did cruelly.

Sex with your partner may also be complicated due to resentment you might feel toward him for "allowing" you to be raped in the first place. You may blame him for not being with you to protect you at the time of the rape. This is especially true if he was supposed to be with you but was not because he was late, was out with his friends or had stormed off in anger after a fight.

Your partner's sexual feelings after your rape may also be complicated and negative. Many men find that they do in fact blame the victim for being raped. This may cause them to question their own sexual abilities. "I must not be good enough if she had to do that." Such blame and self-consciousness may mean that your partner is the one who avoids sexual encounters with you, even though you might be willing.

Likewise, he may come to view you differently as a result of your new status as rape victim. Some men say that they think of their partners as less desirable, and become uninterested in sexual activity. Although it is rare, a few men say that they are sexually aroused by the new status. These are obviously serious and deep-seated sexual responses that you and your partner will have to resolve if you are to have a good sexual relationship in the future.

Many men today, fortunately, are discarding the myths and false assumptions which led men in the past to react to a rape victim in the negative terms described above. This is a tremendous advancement, for rape victims certainly do not need the extra burden such attitudes place on them. Even the enlightened man, however, may suffer from sexual inhibitions in response to rape. If you are raped, your partner may love and support you, but still be afraid to reach out to you sexually. He may fear hurting you or pressuring you. He may be concerned that the type of sex the two of you enjoyed before the rape will now seem too aggressive or violent. These fears may seem like sexual rejection to you, even though in reality your partner is simply trying to make you feel better.

The main solution to your sexual differences is to be found, again, in communication. Talk about your feelings and fears as much as possible. Tell each other how you feel, without being cruel. You certainly do not need to hear that you are suddenly "unclean" in the eyes of your partner; this is something he should discuss with a friend or counselor. But other, less threatening feelings and emotions should be aired so that they do not become built up out of proportion.

One of the most positive things you can do toward resuming sexual relations is to talk specifically about sex. How do you feel when he suggests sex, or pushes you toward it? How could he word his suggestion in a way that you might find more acceptable? Look for cues that remind you specifically of the rape, and talk about alternatives you can explore which eliminate such cues. For example, if your partner uses an expression during sex that reminds you of your rapist, let this be known to him. If you and your partner always enjoyed oral sex with each other until the rapist demanded the same of you, try avoiding oral sex with your partner for awhile until you feel more at ease.

Your partner may make similar suggestions to you; things you might do or say to alleviate some of his concerns. Certainly if you are comfortable with his suggestions, pursue them. Do not do anything that might make you feel worse, however. Remember, you have the right to recover from the crime of rape in your own way. You may choose to compromise, *but you were raped, not your partner, so your needs come first.*

Another way to overcome any sexual problems you may have as a result of rape is to assume the position of sexual initiator more frequently. You choose the time and the place for sex, rather than your partner. This accomplishes two things. First, it affords you the opportunity to be in sexual control; something you could not do during the rape. Proving to yourself that you can resume control is often very therapeutic. Second, it allows you the time you need to rebuild your trust in men. Maybe you just want someone to hold you, or maybe you want sex. Finding out that you can trust your partner to give you what *you* want, and not what he wants, goes a long way toward putting your sex life back on a healthy footing.

If sexual problems persist, you and your partner may want to talk to a trained marriage counselor or sex therapist. A professional may be able to help your sex life by encouraging communication between the two of you. Moreover, the counselor will be able to inform you and your partner about the nature of rape, how it affects relationships and that your problem is not unusual. Sometimes simply learning what you can realistically expect from each other sexually is very helpful. Finally, a counselor can explore with your partner any deep-seated problems he has as a result of your rape; problems which should not be a burden to you but still need to be resolved by your partner.

Remember, sex with your partner will more than likely be satisfying again. It may take time, patience and work, but together you can solve your sexual problems. You may find that the dialogue about sex brings you closer than ever before.

Rape is violence, and not sex. Once you and your partner understand this, the rape should not alter your sexual relationship any more than it alters any other facet of your relationship. You can recover from rape; sexually, and in every other way.

Some Special Considerations

The term partner has been used to describe any close male associate, ranging from a male friend to a husband of many years. Obviously there is a difference in the nature of the relationship from one to the other. The discussion above was geared primarily for a very close and permanent relationship. What if your partner is new to your life and you are only considering a permanent commitment? Will a relationship not yet cemented survive the trauma of rape? This is a difficult question, of course, and only you can determine the answer. It is highly recommended that you take sufficient time after the rape before making any far-reaching decisions. After being raped, it is often tempting to cling to an emotional "lifeboat" rather than face life alone. But take the time to decide if that lifeboat might not really be an anchor. You need not commit yourself to someone who is going to blame you for your rape. You are *not* a different person as a result of the rape. You are neither unclean nor at fault. If your current friend does not understand this, be assured that someone else will someday.

The discussion above has been directed toward male partners. If you and your partner are both women, it is hoped that this chapter will have general relevance for you as members of a relationship. Some of your emotions, however, may be unique. For example, lesbian women may recover from rape more quickly than heterosexual women. Female partners may share more common ground as they face rape recovery. They may be able to empathize with each other and express feelings in that they do not come from separate male/female worlds. If you are raped, and your female partner is there to help you recover, you may face fewer problems than do some other women. It is also helpful to know that your local rape crisis center may address the needs of lesbian victims as part of their services.

A third special consideration applies to women who have no partner now, nor have ever had in the past. If you are a virgin at the time of an attack, you may face some special fears. If your introduction to what appears to be sexuality is terrifying, you may wonder what *real* sexual experiences are like. Remember, rape is not sex. The sexual intimacy you may someday share with someone else will be altogether different from your attack. It will be warm and loving and kind, and that makes it something other than what you experienced. Try to learn the facts about love-making from a good friend, a counselor or a reliable written resource. This will help you to see the difference between rape and sex. Find someone with whom you can discuss any fears you might have. This too will help you to resolve any confusion about the difference between rape and sex.

Telling Your Children

A question rape victims very often have to face is whether or not to tell their children that they were raped. This is never easy, for there is always the concern that children will become overly frightened by a world in which such a thing could happen to their mother. Only you can make the ultimate decision to tell, or not to tell, your children that you have been raped. Only you can decide what details are important to share with them. However, there are some guidelines that might be of help in making these decisions.

Whether or not you choose to tell your children that you were raped will depend upon a number of factors. One of the most important factors is whether or not other people know you have been raped. Rumors have a way of spreading very quickly, and children have a way of eventually hearing these rumors. Keep this in mind as you decide to tell your children. It is much better that they hear of the rape directly from you, or perhaps from your partner, than to overhear it being discussed at a relative's house or to be informed of it on the school playground. If they hear about the rape second hand, they may hear a more frightening and distorted version than if you tell them about it yourself, coolly and calmly.

Another thing to bear in mind is that children quickly sense family upheaval. They know if someone is unhappy, angry or depressed even though it may be "hidden" from them. It may be better to tell your children that you have been raped and that things around the house might be uncomfortable for a while. Children, like adults, have an easier time coping with the known than with the unknown.

Finally, make your decision to tell your children about your rape based on what *you* can handle. If you find it impossible to talk about it with them, or if you think you will do more harm than good, then you may decide to say nothing. One alternative you might consider is to ask their father, a good friend, your family physician or some other capable and trusted adult to explain it to them for you.

If you decide that your children should be told, then you must determine what to tell them. Again, you will have to find your own words, based on what you know about your own children. As you prepare to talk with your children about your rape, you may find it helpful to bear in mind the suggestions which are offered below:

- Share more or less detail with your children depending on their ages. A fourteen-year old can process more information than can a four-year old. Never tell your children more than they want to know. Explain what happened honestly and straight-forwardly, but let your children ask if they want to know more.

- Explain what happened carefully so as not to frighten your children. You may want simply to say that you were attacked by a man who hurt you, but that you can recover. You need not go into every detail about what you were forced to do or how you were hurt in the course of the rape.

- Although you may want to avoid details, still be honest with your children. If they are left uncertain about what happened to you, and then they hear the word "rape," they may imagine something totally false. Tell them that the man forced you to engage in a violent act that involved your body and his. For example, you might say, "He forced me to touch his penis." Choose your words carefully, based on what your children already know about sex. Rape should *not* be their first course in sex education.

- Remind your children that they should feel free to ask you any questions they may have concerning your attack, feelings within the family, comments their friends may make or any other problems which might arise.

- Tell your children that what happened to you has nothing to do with adult sexuality. Remind them that love and love-making are wonderful things. What happened to you was totally different. You may want to liken your rape to being hit or beaten in a playground fight. Such behavior is mean and violent, and has nothing to do with love or affection.

Most importantly, tell your children that you will all be fine again, even though for awhile they might expect some changes in the family. Tell them to be patient, and not to worry. You may want to remind them that you love them very much, even though you might seem a little distant for awhile.

7

If You Know The Rapist

Each year, thousands of women are raped by someone they know, trust, perhaps even love. The crime of rape goes beyond being accosted in the middle of the night by a dreaded stranger. Some women are raped, instead, by a neighbor, a date, their husband's best friend, even their husband.

We knew very little about so-called "acquaintance rape" until recently. Being raped by a known person was even more of a "closet" crime than rape by a stranger. Fortunately, this is changing. Victims of acquaintance rape are starting to talk about what has happened to them and are offering suggestions for surviving this special kind of tragedy. If you are raped by someone you know, you no longer have to endure the crime in silence.

One of the most surprising and frightening facts we have learned about acquaintance rape over the past few years is that it is *the* most common kind of rape. It is thought that well over one half of all rapes are committed by men who are known by their victims. We have no way of being certain about the prevalence of this crime simply because acquaintance rape is much less likely to be reported to the authorities than is stranger rape. We can only guess at the extent of this form of rape. All of the best guesses suggest that acquaintance rape is at least slightly more common than stranger rape, perhaps two or three times more common. This is one of the reasons for devoting a special chapter to this subject.

Another reason for paying special attention to acquaintance rape is that it is a somewhat different crime from stranger rape. Certainly many of the problems and emotions following acquaintance rape mirror those following rape by a stranger. All of the chapters in this book, therefore, will have relevance for rape victims regardless of whether or not their attacker is known to them. Yet, victims of acquaintance rape face a unique set of problems which deserves special consideration. This is not meant to imply that acquaintance rape is more or less serious than other types of rape. *Any* rape is horrifying and traumatic. Acquaintance rape may, however, lead to additional sets of worries and fears which are not experienced by the victims of stranger rape.

Four Stories of Acquaintance Rape

What exactly do we mean by acquaintance rape? How many types of acquaintance rape are there, and how do they differ from each other? Certainly being raped by a casual friend is different from being raped by a husband of many years. No two relationships are ever identical. Therefore, no two acquaintance rapes are ever quite the same. It would be impossible to catalog all of its various forms. In this chapter we will discuss four general kinds of acquaintance rape. Fictitious stories will be told to demonstrate the kinds of situations which might involve acquaintance rape. If you are raped by an acquaintance, your story will no doubt vary to some degree from those discussed below. It is hoped, however, that enough similarities will exist to enable you to understand the crime committed against you.

A Casual Friend

Linda has gone to the same gas station for years. She commonly sees Kenneth working there. He is always friendly, and they have exchanged pleasant words on several occasions. On her way home from work one evening, Linda stops to buy gas. No one is around except Kenneth. He tells her that he has noticed a problem with her car and suggests she drive it into the service area. She follows his suggestion. Once she is alone with him in the garage, he rapes her.

If you find yourself in a situation similar to Linda's, you will face an unusual set of concerns. Beyond your reaction to having been raped, you may question yourself in other ways. Your judge of character is at issue here. How could you have been so wrong about this man? What about the other people with whom you come into contact? Can you trust the grocer, the man at work, your mail carrier?

It is very normal for women who have been raped by a casual acquaintance to question their ability to distinguish violent from non-violent people. Trust becomes a rare commodity as a result. This problem is not as severe if you are raped by a stranger whom you can label a rare "madman." If the rapist appears to be just like other men, you might either assume that everyone is cruel or that you have no skills for identifying persons with whom you can be safe.

Remember, there is no way to know in advance if a man will rape or not. Do not blame yourself if someone who seems trustworthy turns out to be a rapist.

A Date

Nancy goes to a party where she meets an attractive and interesting man. She is pleased when he takes the time to phone her the next day to invite her on a date. It is decided that she will go to his house for a gourmet meal. After dinner, the two sit on the couch and kiss. Suddenly, his advances become more aggressive. She tries to "laugh it off" without seeming rude or frightened. He ignores her rejection and rapes her.

If you are in a situation similar to Nancy's, you too may face some unique problems. Again, the trauma of rape is real enough. You may also find yourself questioning your ability to judge character. It might become difficult to trust any subsequent dates as a result.

In addition, you may wonder whether or not you actually caused the rape by kissing or "petting" with the man in the first place. After all, you did flirt with him and enjoy his embraces. You may wonder if you are not in fact a "tease," someone who brings out the worst in a man by "leading him on." What if you really wanted to be attacked? Such questions about your own behavior, and your own morality, may deepen your sense of guilt following the attack.

Remember, your actions and behaviors do not cause a man to rape. If you flirt, kiss or "pet" with a man, that is your privilege. It does not give anyone the justification to rape you.

A Good Friend

Carmen and her husband have known Wayne and his wife for years. They live in the same neighborhood, attend the same parties and get together for cards. Wayne is like a brother to her, and probably the best friend her husband has. One afternoon Wayne stops by to borrow something and comes inside for a drink. He makes a joke about being alone together, and she jokes back that now is the time to have a fling. His flirtation becomes more serious, and she tries in a lighthearted fashion to make him leave. He refuses; then rapes her.

If you are raped by a good friend, you will have many special issues confronting you. In your own mind, you may question what you did to bring out this side of a man's personality. If you think he has never done anything like this before, you may conclude that it must have been something you did or said to turn him into an "animal." Again, you may wonder if you in fact secretly wanted to be attacked by the friend, especially if you have ever innocently fantasized about him in the past. You also may come to distrust other friends for fear of what they might do to you.

Moreover, you might fear that your other acquaintances will learn of the rape. You might wonder what they will think of you, if and when they know. If your mutual friends appear to be choosing sides over this issue, you may feel caught in the middle of a war you did not try to start. You may wonder if your partner believes your version of what happened, or his friend's. If your partner asks what you were doing alone with the man in the first place, or reminds you of the time you danced with the man at a party, you might feel doubly accused.

Remember, no one has the right to rape you. Moreover, no one has the right to blame you if you are raped.

A Lover

Lynn has been married to the same man for several years. They have always enjoyed a close relationship and a good sex life. Recently he has seemed a changed man. He is irritable, away from home a lot and drinking too much. In the middle of a fight, he starts to approach her sexually. She is too angry to feel desire, and pushes him away. He persists, despite her protests, and rapes her.

Women who are raped by their husbands or lovers often find recovery extremely difficult. This is a very severe form of attack leading to a host of confusing emotions. You may feel that the rape calls into question your judge of character; this is someone you love, someone to whom you have committed your life. Does that mean there is something wrong with you? You may feel guilty, as if you must have done something to force him to act in such a way. You may try to believe that a man you love could not do such a thing unless he was pushed beyond all limits and therefore the rape must be your fault. You may even think he has a "right" to treat you that way, and worry about future encounters. Most importantly, you may feel you do not want to lose someone you love. Even though he has attacked you, you still love him and do not want to face life without him.

Remember, despite your actions, no one, not even your husband, has the right to rape you.

Acquaintance Rape

The unique feelings described above account, in part, for the difficulty some victims face following acquaintance rape. Another reason is that victims often fear confiding in anyone about what has happened to them. If you have been raped by someone you know, you might wonder if your friends and family will blame you. They might question what you were doing to get yourself into a situation leading to rape. Whether we like it or not, the truth is that rape victims receive more sympathy if they are bruised and battered by a total stranger. A shadow of a doubt about your character may exist if the rapist was known to you. This is unfair, obviously, but remains the reality at this point in time. Hopefully this will change as we learn more about acquaintance rape.

Your friends and family might be even less responsive to your pleas for help if they themselves know and like the rapist. They do not want to believe they are bad judges of character any more than you do. They may choose to think that in actuality this was mutually agreed upon sex, blown out of proportion or regretted after the fact.

Turning to the police for support may also seem like a futile gesture. Many victims of acquaintance rape complain that the police are quick to label their cases "unfounded" and send them home. Some unenlightened police officers might actually believe that women deserve to be raped if they start something (such as kissing or petting) with a man. "You got yourself into this mess, now you get yourself out" is an all too common mentality among law enforcement authorities. Others may question the truthfulness of the complaint. Some officers believe that most often a cry of rape-by-a-known-assailant is really nothing more than a woman getting back at a man for a lovers' spat. Given time, they say, she will cool down and the two people will "kiss and make up."

More knowledgeable police officers may still dismiss a case of acquaintance rape, even though they believe it occurred. Acquaintance rape is difficult to prove in a court of law and the officers may not want to spend time on a case which might not result in conviction. As is often true with acquaintance rape, evidence may be scarce so it becomes a matter of your word against his.

Finally, in many areas one form of acquaintance rape is not considered illegal. At present, only a few laws include forcible sexual conduct by a husband in the category of rape.[1] No legal authorities are willing to pursue your case if what your husband did is, in fact, legal behavior.

The crime of acquaintance rape is a horrifying social problem. We are just beginning to understand how it affects victims, and what can be done about it. Changes are starting to be made. It is becoming easier to prosecute cases of acquaintance rape as more legal authorities begin to view it as a serious offense. We need to see acquaintance rape as serious; every bit as intolerable as stranger rape. No woman should be forced to engage in sexual acts with *any* man.

---

[1]Your local rape crisis center will be able to inform you about the legal status of this form of rape in your area. However, even if you cannot prosecute your husband legally, you may still be eligible for rape counseling services and support. Ask your local crisis center about the availability of services in your area.

If you are raped by someone you know, it will be helpful for you to remember several important points:

- *Remember, rape is not less serious just because you were previously acquainted with the person who raped you.*

  A common fallacy is that when a woman is raped by someone she knows, it is somehow less serious than when she is raped by a stranger. Even if you had voluntary sexual relations with the man before you were raped, rape is still rape, and it is serious. Rape occurs *any* time a man forces a woman to comply with his demands against her will.

- *Remember, just because you were raped by someone you know does not mean that you are a poor judge of character.*

  Most rapists do not fit any particular pattern in the way they look or behave. There is no way to know who is likely to rape. Rapists come from all walks of life and have all kinds of personalities. It is not your fault if a friend or neighbor who seemed like "such a nice guy" turns out to be a rapist.

- *Remember, when a person you thought was a nice guy turns out to be a rapist, do not blame yourself or think that you are the cause of his unacceptable behavior.*

  Anyone who would rape you, regardless of the circumstances, is cruel, violent and in the wrong. While every situation is different, do not forget:

  - A woman who is friendly to her neighbor, even invites him in for coffee, does not cause a rape.

  - A woman who kisses a date, even though she has no intention of pursuing further sexual activity, does not cause a rape.

- A woman who gets angry and says something spiteful to her husband or boyfriend, does not cause a rape.

• *Remember, you have the right to be treated with respect.*

No matter what the law says, no one has the right to rape you, not even your husband. Even if you believe you are not the world's best wife, no behavior on your part gives your husband the right to "punish" you by raping you. If your differences cannot be ironed out in a rational manner, you have the right to a life which is more healthy and happy. There are many resources available to you today that have never existed before. Such resources can help you find a way out of a violent and intolerable situation. Shelter houses for abused women, job training programs and counseling services may provide you with the support you need to get yourself, and your children, away from an abusive situation.

• *Remember, most people can still be trusted.*

Perhaps the most difficult thing about being raped by someone you know is that as a result you have difficulty trusting anyone else. Keep in mind that *most* people are trustworthy. They want to make your life better, not worse. You can still trust your judgment of people. You need not totally shut out the world because you have been raped by someone you know.

A great many women have been victimized by acquaintance rape. Even people who have not had this happen to them are on your side. This means that there are thousands of people who are there to support you. Turn to those who understand what you are experiencing. If you can think of no one among your friends and associates, call your rape crisis center. Groups of victims are coming together to talk about their experiences with acquaintance rape. Your rape crisis center may be able to put you in touch with such groups. It helps to discuss your feelings with other people who share your concerns. These people exist and are willing to help. *You are not alone.*

8

Medical Attention

Every woman needs to take time to consider what she will do if she is raped. Certainly, none of us likes to think about the possibility of being raped. Yet most of us do take the time to work out an escape route from our homes or apartments in case of fire. We set up plans or precautions in case of emergency in our everyday lives. Rape is an unexpected, terrible emergency. Every woman should have some idea what to do and what to expect if it occurs. In this chapter we will discuss the kind of medical attention you should seek and what medical procedures you might expect, if you are raped. The last part of this chapter will provide some suggestions about how to prepare yourself in case rape should happen to you.

Why Seek Medical Help?

If you have been raped, it is important that you receive medical attention immediately. The main reason, of course, is to ensure that any injuries caused by the rape are treated. These may include injuries of which you are not aware. *Seek medical help even if you do not plan to report the rape to the police.* You will need medical attention for a number of reasons:

- Rape is a violent crime which is an assault on your physical and emotional well-being. Any injuries resulting from such assault need prompt medical care. You may even have internal injuries of which you are unaware.

- Hospitals often have special rape trauma teams to treat rape victims, and to provide counseling and other forms of follow-up care.

- Immediately after being raped many women say they do not care about prosecuting their attacker.[1] However, it is not at all uncommon to reconsider this issue and later decide to prosecute. Seeking medical attention as soon as possible after the rape will help to maintain your option to prosecute. This is because the evidence collected as part of your medical examination will be used, along with other evidence, to help locate and convict your attacker. The stronger the medical evidence against your rapist, the better your chances of seeing him successfully convicted for his crime. Strong medical evidence is made possible by a prompt and thorough medical examination.

- Seeking medical help after your attack demonstrates to yourself and others that you realize the seriousness of what has happened to you. This will help to show the police and other authorities that your attack is real.

There is also a less obvious reason for seeking medical help. Some research has shown that those victims who receive medical attention feel emotionally better about themselves than do those who avoid treatment. It might be that in seeking medical treatment, you help to convince yourself of the seriousness of what has happened to you, and as such, are less likely to feel ashamed or guilty as much as you feel angry and violated.

---

[1]In this discussion, as well as in the following two chapters, a great deal will be said about prosecuting your attacker. Invariably serious questions arise as women begin to think about rape prosecution. Questions include: "Can I receive medical attention without being required to prosecute?" "If I call the police, does this mean that I have to prosecute?" "What if I decide to prosecute, and then later change my mind?" Prosecution procedures vary tremendously from one area to the next. It is a good idea to know in advance what you might face. Call your rape crisis center, your prosecuting attorney's office or your local police station with your questons. Appendix B will help you in this effort. *Find out immediately if and when you will be required to take legal action against your rapist.*

If you are raped, it is important that you seek help. Start by calling the police, an ambulance, the hospital, your doctor or a friend or relative. Unless you need to treat yourself due to some immediate danger (such as excessive bleeding which might require the application of a bandage, direct pressure or removal of clothing to apply first aid), *do not change anything concerning your appearance. Do not change your clothes, take a shower, brush your teeth or wash any part of your body. Do not even comb your hair or brush your clothing.* This is very important because even though your health always comes first, any change in your physical appearance before you are treated by medical personnel can destroy evidence which may lead to the arrest and conviction of your attacker. We will discuss why this is true later in this chapter.

Getting to the Hospital

If you are at all uncertain about whether or not you can get to a hospital, request an ambulance, a police car or a friend or relative to take you. There is no need to further your misery by being involved in a traffic accident, especially when many governmental jurisdictions provide special services for victims of rape and assault. You may want to ask for an ambulance with a crew trained in rape crisis. Often the hospital will send someone with such training, usually a female nurse. If this is not the case where you live, you may still find that the ambulance crew is more than willing to pay special attention to your needs.

You may want a friend or police officer to accompany you in the ambulance to make sure that any treatment you receive on your way to the hospital minimizes the possibility of destroying evidence of your rape. You might also want to ask that the ambulance crew radio ahead to have the hospital call a friend, relative or rape crisis advocate to meet you when you arrive. Sometimes, but unfortunately not always, you can ask that the ambulance crew take you to a hospital or medical center specializing in rape victim treatment. In any event, it does no harm to request what you want.

Many local police departments also have special rape crisis teams. Take time to find out if this is true in your area. Even if this is not so, you may ask that a policewoman, an officer with rape victim experience or a plain clothes officer accompany you or meet you at the hospital. Remember, regardless of the circumstance, you have a right to receive proper attention. Feel free to ask questions at any time.

What to Expect

The kind of medical attention each person who is raped will receive depends upon the nature of her injuries, the medical procedures used in each hospital and the particular doctors and nurses seen. Generally, however, you can expect the following steps to be taken:

- Upon arrival, you will be requested to complete admissions and medical history forms. Read them carefully before you sign anything. Ask questions if there are any sections you do not understand. Some forms and questionnaires may be completed at a later time.

- You may have to wait in the emergency room before being treated. This is because the primary responsibility of the hospital staff is to attend to the people with the most serious injuries first. The length of your wait will therefore depend, in part, upon how seriously you have been injured and upon how many other emergency cases need attention. Moreover, the examination itself may be lengthy. Most hospitals now use special rape evidence collection kits which require that any evidence obtained by medical personnel be carefully collected and placed in individual containers. Special documents must be completed describing the evidence and your treatment. Expect to be in the hospital for several hours!

- When you see the doctor or nurse, you will be asked questions about your current health, just as you would for any other visit to a doctor or hospital. You will be examined and treated for any bruises, cuts, burns or other wounds.

- You will be asked several personal questions about your sexual behavior. The information you provide helps the medical staff to assess the extent of your injuries, and also to gather evidence. Such questions may include: "When did you last have intercourse?" "When did you last menstruate?" "What form of birth control, if any, do you use?" "Are you currently pregnant?" "Are you currently suffering from any infections or venereal diseases?"

- A pelvic examination will follow. Some victims find this especially uncomfortable after their recent experience. However, it is necessary to evaluate any possible damage to the vagina, cervix or genital area. It is also necessary for the collection of evidence. Oral and anal examinations and treatment may also be performed. Any specimens relating to the rape will be collected and marked for future legal processing. If you plan to prosecute, these exams are important. For example, even if you are sure ejaculation did not occur, some leakage of semen still might be detected and used to help identify your assailant. Or, even in a case where no oral sex took place, an examination of the mouth may still provide bits of the attacker's hair, clothing fibers or other helpful clues. All of these pieces of evidence help to link the attacker to the crime.

- Blood and urine samples will be taken. This is necessary to test for pre-existing pregnancy or venereal disease. In the process, many different health problems can be identified by the blood test. The blood test is also important for evidence gathering. Samples of your blood can be used to identify blood stains on the attacker's clothing, or to tell the difference between his blood and yours on your own clothing.

- Blood and urine samples may be tested for alcohol or other drugs in your system. This may be one of the measures taken to assess whether or not you are being honest about your attack. For example, later in court your rapist's lawyer might try to convince a jury that you had been drinking excessively at the time of your attack and therefore cannot be trusted to remember minute details of what happened. You may have the right to decide whether the results of any such tests should be released to the police. You may also have to sign forms allowing the results to be transferred to the authorities. Do not neglect to ask questions about any such tests. Remember, too, that if you used any drugs or drank any alcohol *after* the attack, as a means to calm down, you should make this known to medical personnel.

- Head, pubic combings and fingernail scrapings will be taken. This is necessary to collect any foreign substances which might be useful as evidence. These include bits of the attacker's skin, blood, hair, clothing fibers, even dandruff. Again, such examinations may also provide important health information.

- Medical personnel may take some or all of your clothing as evidence. If it is ripped or torn, it may be marked as evidence for use in court to show that you resisted the force used upon you. The attacker's blood or other secretions might be present in the fabric. You may have picked up some identifiable residue from the scene of the crime, the attacker's home, auto or office. Be sure to ask a friend or relative to bring a change of clothes for you in the event that some or all of your clothing is retained as evidence. A rape crisis center advocate or even the hospital staff might also provide you with something to wear.

You Have Medical Rights

If at any time you feel you are not being properly treated, that evidence is being mishandled or that any medical problems are being overlooked, by all means make this known to those attending you, or if necessary, to their supervisor(s). Here are some things of which you should be aware as you receive treatment:

- If the attending physician fails to examine you for specific injuries (such as might result from anal intercourse, for example), and you know such injuries are a possibility, be sure to make the physician aware of them.

- Many hospitals have specially trained doctors, nurses and staff for the treatment of rape victims. Sometimes, a hospital or medical center will have a special waiting room and/or emergency entrance for rape and assault victims. This can be very helpful if you feel conspicuous sitting in a waiting room with other patients. Ask about the special services available to you.

- You have the right to be accompanied by a friend, relative or a trained advocate. You may want to ask the hospital staff to call someone for you. The person can be with you through the examination if you so desire.

- In some areas, medical professionals are required by law to notify the police if they treat a victim of a serious crime. In other areas, you retain the right to notify the police yourself. Either way, you may be asked to sign a form allowing any medical evidence to be released to the police. The evidence will then aid in the arrest and conviction of your rapist. However, the decision to release medical evidence is usually yours. *Be sure to ask about such procedures in your area.*

- You have the right to exclude male police officers from the room during your physical examination. If an officer needs to be present for legal reasons, you may request a female officer.

- Often the police will want photographs of any injuries you received as a result of your rape. These photos may be used as evidence that force was used against you. They may also be used by the police for comparison with other victims with similar injuries to determine if your attacker is responsible for more than one crime. You have the right to request that any photographs be taken by a female nurse, police woman or medical staff member. You also have the right to refuse to be photographed. Remember, however, that the photos may be helpful in the prosecution of your rapist.

- You have the right to keep your rape out of the news media. If this is your desire, as is so often the case, inform the hospital staff when you are admitted.

- If you have a pre-existing medical condition which you feel might damage your credibility, ask that the attending doctor or nurse note this condition on a form separate from the one used to record rape evidence. For example, if you received treatment for drug addiction prior to being raped, this should *only* be recorded on a separate form, if at all. Only information which is relevant to the rape itself should be collected for police officials.

- You have the right to change your mind and refuse treatment. You also have the right to ask about the medical and legal consequences of your treatment. Finally, you have the right to leave the hospital at any time.

- Many governments now provide monetary compensation for medical expenses incurred by a victim for treatment of injuries related to sexual assault (see Chapter 10). Ask that a hospital staff person show you how to apply for compensation if such a program exists in your region.

After Leaving the Hospital

At some point you will be released from the hospital, provided your physical injuries are not serious enough to warrant a longer stay. You may not want to be alone, or at least not go home alone. Ask that a friend, police officer or advocate take you home. You may even have the police check your house and neighborhood. If it makes you feel more comfortable, you may want to stay with a friend or family member. Some rape crisis centers have temporary shelters for women who fear returning home soon after a rape experience.

Any pregnancy or venereal disease which may occur as a result of your being raped cannot be detected immediately. Therefore, *make sure that you are rechecked by medical professionals for these possibilities not more than six weeks after you are attacked.* Surprisingly, some rape victims forget to take this step until such conditions become advanced. You may ask that hospital staff contact you to remind you of the need for further attention. You may want to make a note of it yourself, or have a friend jot it in a calendar or appointment book.

If pregnancy, venereal disease or any other problems arise as a result of rape, treatment of some sort will be necessary. Treatment for pregnancy involves some controversy. For example, should the "morning-after" pill,[1] which terminates a possible pregnancy, be administered in the hospital immediately after a rape occurs?

---

[1] The "morning-after" pill refers to a drug, administered as a tablet or injection, used to terminate a possible pregnancy. The kind or brand of drug you may receive will depend upon area statutes, hospital policy and the clinical judgment of the physician attending you.

Some people believe that the morning-after pill should be prescribed automatically to rape victims. Others feel that drugs of this nature should never be prescribed. Bear in mind that serious medical side effects have been associated with the morning-after pill. These side effects include harm to an embryo or fetus in the case of pre-existing pregnancy as well as harm to the victim herself. You do not need to make any immediate decisions regarding pregnancy termination. Clarify your options with your rape crisis advocate and medical personnel.

Make sure that you ask about any treatments which might be prescribed, why they are necessary and what the possible side effects might be. Counseling may be available in your area if you are unsure of any decisions you have to make regarding medical treatment and follow-up care. Remember, only you can decide what is best for you. It is helpful to obtain as much information as possible before making any decisions.

Important Precautions

Remember, as gruesome as the idea may be, it is good to be prepared[1] in the event that you are raped. You may want to check on the following, write down phone numbers and keep the information handy:

- Investigate your local hospitals and clinics. Some facilities do not have emergency rooms, others specialize in rape crisis. Find out which medical centers have separate waiting rooms for rape victims, kits for rape evidence gathering and medical staff trained in rape victim treatment. There have been incidences of intentional improper evidence gathering during treatment of rape victims by doctors and nurses who do not want to have to testify in court at some later date. For that and other reasons, it is important to know which facility you would like to use before a rape occurs.

---

[1] Further information about being prepared can be found in Appendix B.

- Identify local rape crisis centers. The center of your choice may be a community or religious organization. Both types usually provide helpful information such as which hospitals or clinics handle rape cases and offer emotional counseling, as well as what laws and statutes pertain to rape in your area. Some centers also provide rape crisis volunteers experienced in medical advocacy. Write down the number of the center of your choice in the space provided in Appendix B and keep it handy.

- Write down the phone numbers of people upon whom you can depend to come to your aid. These may be friends or relatives who could bring you a change of clothes in the hospital, take care of your house or provide a place for you to stay.

Whatever choices you make, remember that you should not neglect medical care for any reason, even if you do not think you can afford it. If you do not have hospital or medical insurance, remember that many areas now provide free or low-cost health examinations for people who have been raped. Again, feel free to ask any doctor or nurse or your local rape crisis center about the services available to you.

9

Getting Legal Help

If you are raped, you have a very difficult choice to make. Should you, or should you not, do everything in your power to see that your rapist is prosecuted for what he did to you? Many victims have a difficult time answering this question in the first few hours or days following the crime of rape. This is why it is so important to think about the pros and cons of prosecution now. It is also important to know exactly what you will face, should you decide to try to prosecute. These issues are discussed in the next two chapters. The information provided will make the legal process easier for you, if you are raped.

Why Rape Victims Do Not Report the Crime of Rape

Rape victims are less likely to report the crime than are the victims of other crimes such as burglary or robbery. Some women come to believe that it is their fault that they were raped in the first place. They "prosecute" themselves, not the rapist. Very often, women who have been raped feel that they cannot face the ordeal of legal procedures following the attack. They may feel ashamed or embarrassed. What will people think if they know? How will they be able to tell strangers about the details of the attack? How will their families feel about the decision to take legal action?

A second reason why many women do not report being raped is that they fear the consequences of such action. There is always the possibility that the rapist will retaliate with future attacks on the victim, or the people she loves. If the rapist is released on bail, if he is not convicted, if his sentence is merely a probationary period or if he only serves a short prison sentence, might he not return to cause further trouble? Often a rapist threatens his victim during the attack, telling the woman that he will kill her if she goes to the police.

Certainly a third and important reason why many women do not report rape is that they believe the legal ordeal will be futile. They may feel that the police and other legal professionals will be unresponsive and unconcerned; that nothing will come of their efforts to bring the rapist to justice. Worse than that, they worry that the legal establishment itself will treat them with cruelty and harrassment. Minority women may be especially concerned about being treated improperly by a predominantly white, male legal establishment.

The end result is that many rape victims feel that taking legal action will simply make their situation worse. There are several reasons for this state of affairs, some of which are changing as we learn more and more about the crime of rape. The first and most important reason is that the legal profession itself has believed in rape "myths" every bit as much as other uninformed people. The laws of many countries reflect a belief in these myths. For example, historically women had to prove that they were forced to engage in sexual activity. They had to convince a jury that they fought back, trying hard to save what was theirs—their bodies; their lives. Ironically, no such requirement is necessary for the crime of robbery. A robbed person need not prove that he or she fought to keep money away from the hands of a robber. The assumption is that no one willingly gives money to a stranger, but a woman willingly gives her body to anyone who happens along. (By the way, in many areas the proof of resistance is still necessary for rape prosecution.)

Another myth which is still reflected in some regional laws is that women cause an attack by their "enticing" behavior. Many readers may recall the Wisconsin judge who argued that a young rape victim had "asked for" her attack by dressing in a particularly "sexy" fashion. There is a fear in the legal establishment that women cry rape after the fact when a desire for sexual activity was their initial motivation. Women victims are seen as fulfilling a fantasy and then labeling it rape out of spite, anger or a play for attention. This has meant that women have had to prove that they did not want the rape, and that they did not consent to it. In its extreme form, it has meant that women have had to prove that they are "good" women who in no way agreed to be taken by a rapist.

Women, in other words, have suffered, and continue to suffer, from society's distrust of their accusations. The image of a vindictive, lying woman trying to get back at a man is very much a cornerstone of the legal processing of rape cases. Unlike victims of other crimes, the rape victim faces moral evaluations, behavioral judgments and distrust. This is changing slowly, but certainly we cannot say at this time that the crime of rape receives the same treatment as any other crime. A woman should still expect to face a unique set of responses if she reports the rape and attempts to prosecute her attacker. She may have to prove that she was forced to comply and that she tried to resist the attack. She may have to be able to corroborate her story. (This means that she may need to be able to confirm what happened by means of evidence beyond her word alone.)

It should be pointed out that this necessary proof may be quite difficult to obtain. Many researchers have studied rape cases to determine what factors influence what is considered to be "enough" proof. As might be expected, rape is difficult to prove if the victim is considered distrustful. The victim is therefore evaluated for what is seen as her credibility or use of good judgment. Unfortunately, these character evaluations are often decided by factors which should have nothing to do with the determination of rape. Questions such as, ''Was the victim hitchhiking?'' ''What was she wearing?'' ''Was she bruised and battered indicating that force was used against her?'' are common, but inappropriate. Race, age, marital status and psychological health of victims have also been found to be linked to perceived credibility or trustworthiness. Moreover, some research shows that women are seen as less credible if they are obese or considered plain and unattractive. The poor, single, young woman is often seen as less credible than the married, middle-aged, ''pillar of the community.'' Women who receive welfare, for example, are less likely to be taken seriously than women who hold prestigious jobs or are the wives of prominent men. Obviously, the legal perception of rape may be complicated and biased. All of this makes the decision to report the crime of rape a very difficult one to make.

Why Rape Victims Do Report the Crime of Rape

In light of these concerns, why do some women still report the crime to the police? One reason is that many victims find the process of reporting the rape and working toward prosecuting the rapist to be quite helpful and supportive. This may seem surprising until one considers that a certain sense of self-worth may emerge from taking legal action. Some claim that they find a great deal of satisfaction in the knowledge that they are attempting to protect themselves, and other women in the community, from future suffering. Trying to put their rapist behind bars helps some victims put the attack in the past.

Moreover, many claim that the process of taking legal action is a good way to release pent-up emotions. The telling and re-telling of the events of the rape can bring such emotions out in the open, making them objective and more manageable. It is an opportunity for *victims* to be in charge, not rapists. This is a very satisfying posture for rape victims to assume.

Another reason why some women now report being raped is that the legal institution is changing in this regard. From the initial police contact all the way to the courtroom, the legal process is becoming more and more supportive of rape victims. Many positive changes in the legal system have emerged over the past several years making rape prosecution today a much more positive experience for victims.

Remember, the initial decision to report your rape to the police should be yours alone. It will not be an easy decision by any means. Risks do exist. The rapist may be found innocent. You may be treated without compassion or concern. If you are raped, you will have to face this decision. Bear in mind two positive notes as you make this important choice concerning whether or not to take legal action:

- Legal action may, in fact, help you in your emotional recovery.

- The better prepared you are to engage in the process of prosecuting your attacker, and the more you know about what to expect, the easier the process will be.

Research has shown that informed women are both more likely to report the crime of rape, and more likely to see the prosecution reach a successful conclusion. That is, they are more likely to see their attacker punished. The rest of this chapter is devoted to the first part of the legal process, notifying the police. In the next chapter you will learn about the exact steps involved in prosecuting your rapist.

The Legal Process Varies

Mention should be made of a particular problem arising for rape victims. Each geographic area has its own laws regarding the crime of rape. Moreover, each area has its own particular procedures for law enforcement and for taking legal action. What is given here, therefore, is only a general idea of what to expect. The discussion which follows will closely approximate your local system, although the specific process in your area may be slightly different. You are encouraged to learn more about how the crime of rape is treated in your own area. Even if you have not been raped, it is helpful to know what to expect. You may want to check with your local rape crisis center to obtain this information. Certainly you could ask a lawyer about rape processing. Or you may want to call your police station to ask questions about how rape cases are handled. Local public libraries also contain information about area laws and procedures. Any reference librarian will be able to direct you to such information.

The Reporting Process

The police serve as the first contact a rape victim makes with the legal system. Talking to the police will be the initial step you take on the road toward prosecuting your rapist. It is important to talk to the police as soon as possible after your attack. *The sooner you report your rape to the police, the greater your chances of successfully prosecuting your attacker*. Remember that simply reporting your rape to the police will not usually commit you to any further legal requirements. Talking to the police simply maintains your option to prosecute at a later time.

You may choose to call the police immediately from the site of the rape (either from home or from a phone close to the rape location). In this case, you will speak to a police dispatcher. She or he will ask several questions regarding:

- The site of the rape, to determine the exact police department with the proper jurisdiction

- The extent of emergency to determine whether or not an ambulance should be dispatched

- The identity or a description of the rapist and his means of escape

If you do not call the police from the rape site, you may choose to go to the hospital or to a rape crisis center. In this case, the police may be phoned by someone else on your behalf.

When the police arrive, you will be asked to tell your version of the rape for the first time. Remember to be as specific as possible as you recount the events. It is very important that you are accurate with the police at this stage. Quite often, initial statements you make to the police are admissible later in a court of law. The legal philosophy is that victims may in fact be more "truthful" in a time of acute crisis, before they have time to think about the event and fabricate or imagine false details. This philosophy can have serious consequences for rape victims. For example, assume you initially tell the police that you saw a gun in the rapist's hand before the attack. Later, you remember that you were only threatened with the gun, but you did not actually see it until the attack was finished. If you testify to the latter in court, and then your earlier testimony is presented, you may appear deceitful or inconsistent to a jury, thereby damaging your overall credibility. To avoid this problem, you may find it helpful to take some time to collect your thoughts before answering the police officers' questions. If it helps, write down or even tape record the details of the rape. Feel free to ask the police for any supplies (paper, pen, tape recorder) you need. Such notes will help to clarify in your own mind exactly what happened before, during and after the attack. Ask the police officers to give you this brief preparation time. Remember, they too should be interested in the accuracy of what you say.

Another way to safeguard your initial testimony to the police is to ask that they not write down your words verbatim. Again, your initial interview with the police may be admissible in court. During a time of acute stress, you might use slang sexual references, make jokes or relate specific details erroneously. This is normal, but may damage your courtroom credibility later. Ask that police officers write down your initial testimony in their own words rather than quoting you directly. (Later, when you discuss your rape with other court representatives such as police investigators or prosecuting attorneys, you may be quoted verbatim or even tape recorded. This is unavoidable but, luckily, by that time your thoughts will be collected and organized.)

It is common to avoid thinking about rape. However, it is important to clarify the facts immediately in order to prepare for the process of repeating your story to legal authorities. Questions you will want to be able to answer include:

- When and where were you approached by the rapist?

- When and where were you actually raped?

- What did the man look like, what did he wear, did he have any identifying marks, scars or a beard? Was he circumcised or not?

- Do you recall any unusual odor associated with the man such as gasoline or a specific cologne?

- Did you notice any particular speech patterns or slang phrases used by the rapist?

- If you were raped by more than one man, how many attackers were there and what did they say to each other? What names did they use to address each other?

- Was the rapist on foot, using mass transit or driving a car? If he was driving, what was the car's make, model, color, license number and so forth?

- Did you notice the apparent use of drugs, including alcohol?

- What weapons were used, if any, and what kind of struggle took place, if any?

- Exactly what was said by the rapist, and what did you say to him?

- What kind of sexual activity did the rapist specifically demand, and what did he actually obtain?

- Did you notice anything else special or unique about the rapist such as lack of erection, urinating, name-calling and so forth?

This information may lead the police to recognize a similarity between your attacker and a known chronic offender. The police will prompt you for this information by asking questions. Offer as much information as you possibly can. If details occur to you after your initial interview with the police, feel free to add them later. One benefit of writing down or taping the details of the rape is that it allows you the opportunity to review your story during the next few days and weeks. Simply adding to your initial testimony after the rape occurs should not hurt your chance to prosecute the rapist successfully.

Some details of the rape may not be revealed simply because the police do not ask the right questions or look in the right places. You may want to make suggestions to the police to ensure that they know everything about the rape. Tell them exactly where the rapist was, and what he touched. If you are raped at home, do not move anything that the rapist might have disturbed. The police may want to take your fingerprints in order to distinguish yours from the rapist's. They may also ask to photograph any bruises, lacerations or burns you received as a result of the rape.[1] They may want to make a "witness check," asking if anyone saw or heard anything suspicious. Unfortunately, many rape victims complain that they have to do the work for the police by volunteering

---

[1] This procedure is discussed more fully in Chapter 8.

information and making suggestions. Remember, if you feel the police are not being thorough enough, it is to your advantage to request that they do more.

Remember, also, that you may have certain privileges in the eyes of the law. Feel free to request these privileges when you talk to the police. You may ask, for example, that an unmarked car with non-uniformed officers call at your house if you are concerned about your neighbors knowing you were victimized. To ensure your privacy, you may want to request that the police do not call you with follow-up questions at work or at home.

Moreover, you have the right to be treated with respect by the police. Research has shown that victims find recovery more difficult if they are confronted by skeptical, distrustful or rude police officers. Feel free to request a female officer if that makes you feel more comfortable. Some police districts have special rape task forces trained specifically to deal with cases of rape. If the attending officer is acting inappropriately in your estimation, request to speak to another officer. *No* officer has the right to ask irrelevant questions about your rape. A fine line exists between questions which may be embarrassing, yet still helpful for the police investigation, versus questions which are simply intended to degrade the victim. An officer who asks, for example, "How many orgasms did you experience?" is clearly overstepping boundaries. If you are unsure of the relevance of a particular question, feel free to ask why it is important.

You also have the right to ask that a lawyer,[1] spouse, family member, friend or trained advocate be present during the questioning. You may do whatever is most comforting to you under the circumstances, including not being alone with the police.

---

[1]Retaining a private lawyer to assist you in prosecuting the crime of rape is possible, but certainly not necessary. Private legal services are provided at low cost to anyone who cannot afford legal expenses. Remember, you should not *need* a lawyer, but may choose to have one (See Chapter 10).

One final caution should be heeded with regards to the police. Some police officers have a tremendous amount of discretion in the processing of criminal cases. If the attending police officer decides not to pursue your case, you have the right to demand to talk to his or her superior. As you will learn in the next chapter, your case may "drop out" of the system at any point. You still have the right, however, to ask that your case be taken seriously by the police.

The police officer with whom you speak at the time of the rape will probably not be an investigator. It will be necessary for you to go to the police station some time after the actual rape to be interviewed by an investigator or detective. Here you will be asked to tell your story for the second time. You will have had some additional time to think about the events of the rape so that you can be more specific than you were during the initial interview. You may want to take your own notes with you when you speak to the investigator so as not to overlook any small details. (These notes are for your use only and should *not* be turned over to the police.)

You will probably be asked to help in the identification of the rapist if he was unknown to you. This may include looking through mug shots, trying to identify the rapist in a line-up or assisting an artist with a composite drawing. You will also be asked to identify weapons, clothing or any other evidence gathered by the police.

Some rape victims are asked to take a polygraph, or lie detector test. This test is given to determine if a victim can be trusted and believed. The results of the test are not usually admissible in a court of law, but they may be used by legal authorities to decide whether to prosecute or not. Another test of a similar nature is a blood analysis taken immediately after the rape to test for drug content. Many concerned people are working with law enforcement personnel to help them understand the harm such tests can cause victims. As a result, the practice of testing the victim's credibility seems to be decreasing, but it is still a possibility you may face.

One of your rights in the legal process is to refuse such tests. You may simply say that you will not be submitted to a polygraph. The blood analysis tests are conducted by hospital staff. You have the right *not* to allow your blood to be tested for alcohol or other drugs. If your blood is tested for drugs, you have the right *not* to sign any forms which might permit the hospital to give the results of such tests to the police. Two problems arise with such refusal, however. One, the authorities may interpret your refusal as an indication of your own untruthfulness. Second, you may pass up an opportunity to "prove" that you are telling the truth. You may want to consult a lawyer or rape advocate before reaching a decision about such tests. If you think there is a chance that any tests of your credibility will be damaging, you may refuse them.

In addition, you have the right to ask the investigator why she or he is questioning you in a particular way. As mentioned, you can have your own lawyer present when you speak to the investigator or, if you prefer, a trained advocate, friend or family member. You may ask to talk to a different investigator, if one is available, in the event that you believe you are being treated unfairly. Finally, you have the right to talk to the investigator at your convenience. You may want to schedule an appointment at the police station which does not interfere with your work commitments. If you have no transportation to the station, you may ask to be picked up in an unmarked car.

The police officers and investigators with whom you speak should be there to serve you, not harrass you. They will try to find and apprehend your attacker and begin legal action against him. You are usually not legally committed to prosecution procedures until a suspect has been apprehended and has had charges brought against him. Remember, you are simply retaining your option to prosecute until this happens.

Notes of Caution

Before turning to the next steps in the legal process, two notes of caution need to be discussed. First, remember that police terminology can be confusing at best. Feel free to ask for specific explanations of anything you do not understand.[1] Two terms which often confuse and even anger women are "alleged" and "unfounded." Your case may be referred to as the "alleged rape" until the rapist is actually convicted of the crime. This should not be interpreted by you to mean "possible" rape. The term alleged is used by the authorities in order to avoid jeopardizing the case against the rapist. You know you were raped, regardless of how it is discussed by police officers and other court representatives.

"Unfounded" is a term used by the police in some areas to refer to a crime which they choose not to pursue. It is often misinterpreted by victims to mean that the police feel the accusation is false. There are many reasons why legal authorities choose not to pursue a case, most of which are discussed in the next chapter. Regardless of the reason, the case is labeled unfounded. Only rarely, probably less than one percent of the time, is rape falsely accused. This rate is quite similar to that of all other crimes. Do not feel as though you are being thought of as a false accuser simply because your case is determined to be unfounded.

Finally, remember that you will have to be in communication with police officers and investigators on more than one occasion. Record the names, badge numbers and phone numbers of the law enforcement authorities to whom you speak. There is space provided in Appendix B for that purpose. Feel free to call these persons again with follow-up questions and/or additional information as the need arises.

---

[1] A glossary presented in Appendix C may be helpful in explaining those terms with which you are unfamiliar.

10

Taking Legal Action

This chapter is written for those victims of rape who choose to take legal action against their attackers. Many women find taking legal action to be extremely therapeutic; others find it a second kind of hell, especially if the rapist is not convicted. Make sure you decide for yourself whether or not to take legal action.

If you do choose to take action against your attacker, you may find that you are faced with a bewildering criminal justice system. You may never have been a part of any criminal court proceedings. The confusion which results from being confronted with a system you do not understand could diminish your ability to prosecute your attacker successfully. A confused victim does not make a competent witness. The more you know about your legal rights and responsibilities as a victim of rape, the better your chances of seeing your attacker convicted for the crime he committed against you. Therefore it is important for you to understand all that will occur throughout the prosecution. This chapter will help by telling you what to expect and by reminding you of *your* rights as the victim.

Steps in the Legal Process

The following step-by-step description of the legal process will help you to understand your own rights and responsibilities. A problem arises, however, with any such description. Each geographic area has its own separate criminal justice system. This means no two areas are exactly alike in their terminology, legal definitions, criminal processing or sentencing practices. Even though similarities exist, you may find that the legal process in your area is somewhat different from the one described below. If you do not understand specific details, feel free to request any necessary information. The police, the prosecuting attorney or your rape crisis center should be able to provide you with the information you need.

Step One: The Prosecuting Attorney

The prosecuting attorney (sometimes referred to as the district attorney or prosecutor) is the lawyer who represents society, specifically the people of the district in which you live. Although it seems depersonalizing, once the wheels of the criminal justice system are set in motion, you are no longer the only victim of the crime of rape. Rather, all of society is perceived as having been hurt by the crime. This is why you often hear "State v. Jones," rather than the victim's name versus Jones. The whole region is going to court, with the prosecuting attorney as its representative. You are included in the region, of course, and are *represented totally free of charge*. Because of this technicality, you become a witness for the court in addition to being the victim of a crime. You can therefore be subpoenaed to appear in court just like any other witness. As a general rule you become a witness, in addition to a victim, once a suspect has been apprehended and the prosecuting attorney becomes involved in the case. (Be aware that this may cause problems for you as the victim. If you decide to change your mind and not take legal action, you may still be forced to serve as a witness against your rapist. As a general rule, however, prosecutors only proceed in those cases where the victim strongly desires prosecution. Thus, in practice you are usually allowed to change your mind about prosecuting even though you become a witness.)

After the police have arrested a suspect (the presumed rapist), it is their responsibility to file initial charges against him and turn the case over to a prosecuting attorney. The attorney will handle the details of the case from that point forward. Bear in mind that sometimes the police decide they do not have enough information to arrest, book and charge a suspect. If this happens in your case, you may want to go directly to the prosecutor yourself to inform him or her that you have been raped.

Once a suspect has been arrested, the prosecuting attorney will review the case. The attorney will interview you to hear your account of what happened. She or he will decide whether there is ''probable cause'' to assume that this suspect has in fact committed a crime. The prosecutor will be able to build a case against your rapist only if there is probable cause to do so.

Probable cause is a difficult, and often subjective, legal determination. What constitutes probable cause is a complicated matter, and one which varies tremendously from one area to another. Therefore, any discussion here must be general. It is important that you understand the laws in your own area.

One important issue in the determination of probable cause is corroboration. Corroboration is that which confirms other evidence, such as your account of the rape. Evidence proving that a rape actually took place, and that it was committed by this particular rapist, may be necessary. Medical evidence (blood, semen and fingernail scrapings), clothing analyses, a positive identification in a line-up and even an eye witness often provide such corroboration. Evidence of the rapist's opportunity to rape and lack of alibi may also be important.

Sometimes the prosecuting attorney will decide there is not enough evidence to charge the suspect with the crime of rape. Although the attorney may believe your account of what happened, he or she might fear that a judge or jury would not have enough evidence to convict a man of rape. At this point the prosecutor may decide not to bring charges against the suspect at all. Or, she or he may decide to bring a lesser charge against the suspect such as aggravated assault, robbery or attempted rape. This can be very frustrating for victims; invariably lesser charges lead to lighter penalties. Be prepared, a charge other than rape is always a possibility throughout the criminal justice process and it is a practice over which victims have very little control.

Determining probable cause often involves, as has been said, the availability of corroboration. Another factor contributes to whether or not a prosecuting attorney feels there is probable cause. Some courts still require proof that you resisted sexual activity. Evidence of resistance often includes such things as signs of breaking and entering your home or apartment, bruises, scratches, burns, rope marks, torn clothing and the use or threat of weapons. You may have to prove you were forced or coerced into sexual relations and that you tried to resist.

Also, a case is built in accordance with the legal statutes of the area in which you live. For example, being raped by your husband may not be illegal in your area. Homosexual rape or rape which does not include penetration of the genitalia may also be excluded. Moreover, several areas have degrees of severity for the crime of rape. The prosecutor will determine whether or not your assault is legally defined as rape and, if so, how it should be classified.

Additional factors determine whether or not the prosecutor decides your rape can be made into a case for prosecution. Like other people in the criminal justice system (for example, the police, a judge or a grand jury), the prosecuting attorney has discretion. He or she can decide not to prosecute if the evidence above is deemed insufficient. Other factors which may enter into the decision include:

- The conduct of the accused at the time of the arrest

- Lack of motive on your part to lie about the rape

- Your willingness to have the events of the rape examined

- The promptness with which you reported the rape

- Whether you are deemed too young or too upset to be a good witness

- The degree to which you are viewed as a consistent and cooperative witness

Finally, a few other factors have been linked to the determination of probable cause, many of which are biased and unfair. Minority and low-income women are less likely to be taken seriously by the criminal justice system. Moreover, the cases of women who are viewed as "immoral" may be dropped (for example, women who have had prior sexual relations with the rapist, women who have "bad" reputations or women with different or "unusual" living arrangements). Women are less likely to be taken seriously if they are viewed as precipitating the rape. If a woman was drinking in a bar and then went home with a stranger, or if she was hitchhiking, she could be viewed by some as having precipitated her rape.

It cannot be stressed strongly enough that discretion is a part of the criminal justice system. The police and/or the prosecuting attorney may decide not to pursue your rapist due to the reasons listed above. Rape prosecution is difficult under the present system. This, again, is due in part to the inherent distrust of the female accuser. It is also due to a somewhat erroneous perception of juries as being overly sympathetic to rape victims. Many fear that this creates a situation by which innocent men go to prison on the basis of insufficient evidence. Conversely, many officials feel that a jury will never convict a man accused of raping a "tramp," so any proceedings with a questionable witness will prove to be a waste of time. This is an unfair, but unfortunately all too common, situation. The recommendations listed below will help you to avoid these unjust practices:

- Be as straight-forward and confident of your story as possible.

- Always demand to see another court official if you feel you are being treated unfairly.

- Hire your own lawyer or use a trained advocate to help ensure that your rights are protected.

- Ask about any information on file in the prosecutor's office concerning your case. If it is inaccurate, make this known to the attorney.

- Obtain a copy of the police report on your case. Study this report so that you are prepared to discuss any of the details it contains.

- Make suggestions which might help the prosecuting attorney prepare your case such as witnesses who can testify on behalf of your character, evidence overlooked and so forth. Find out if prosecutors investigate crimes themselves, or merely rely on police investigations. If the latter is true where you live, you will want to be especially thorough in your suggestions. Tell the prosecutor everything you know about the crime committed against you so that nothing is inadvertently overlooked.

- If you have any questions, ask the prosecuting attorney.

- Contact local resources if you suspect you are being treated improperly. Those who may help include your local chapter of the National Organization for Women (NOW), Women Against Rape, your YWCA or your rape crisis center.

Step Two: The Initial Appearance

If the prosecuting attorney decides to pursue your case, an initial appearance will be scheduled. This will take place shortly after a suspect has been arrested, usually within 24 hours. There is a good chance you will not have to be present at this appearance. This initial procedure is not a trial. It is simply an opportunity for the suspect to face a court official (often called a magistrate), be given formal notice of the charges against him and be advised of his rights. The magistrate will also decide whether the suspect should be kept in jail awaiting further court action.

Be aware that the suspect may be released at this point. He may be set free on bail, or even be released on his own recognizance (ROR). This means that he is freed temporarily with the promise he will return for future court proceedings. His promise is guaranteed with his money (bail) or simply with his own word (ROR). Many victims find it extremely disturbing to learn that their rapist is walking the streets between the time of the attack and the actual court date. The philosophy behind this practice is that everyone is innocent until proven guilty. Therefore, a potentially innocent man should not be imprisoned until his guilt is thoroughly established. This philosophy is less than comforting if it is your rapist who has been set free. Remember, under no circumstances does your attacker have the right to approach you while he is out on bail. If you see the suspect near your house or place of employment, or if you are contacted by the suspect in any way, even by phone, do not hesitate to call the police.

Step Three: Legal Assistance for the Suspect

The United States criminal justice system is based upon an adversarial model[1] which means that two parties, the state and the accused rapist, compete or argue with each other in a courtroom. The state, represented by the prosecuting attorney, presents your side of the argument. The defense attorney is hired or appointed

---

[1]The adversarial model is not used in all countries. If you live outside the United States, you will want to ask how Step #3 in your country varies from the description herein.

to present the suspect's side of the argument, whether or not the defense attorney believes the rapist is guilty. It is the defense attorney's job to prove you are wrong: that you were not raped at all; that you were raped by a different person; or that you volunteered to participate in sexual activity with the defendant (suspect). In other words, the defense attorney is paid to convince a jury that you are lying, or at least mistaken.

In order to defend the rapist, a defense attorney prepares evidence against you. This may include courtroom evidence presented to diminish your credibility. It may be a witness who saw you voluntarily talking to the rapist. This could be construed as evidence that you did not try to resist and call into question actual sexual activity with the rapist. These courtroom tactics are often frustrating and humiliating. Remember, however, the defense attorney is not *attacking* you as much as she or he is *defending* a client.

In some areas, prosecuting and defense attorneys share information with each other. The reason for this practice is to ensure that neither attorney is faced with unexpected evidence when it comes time for the actual trial. Ask if this practice is followed in your area. If not, you will want to work quite closely with the prosecutor in an effort to ''second-guess'' the defense attorney. Tell the prosecutor anything about yourself that might become an issue in court. For example, was there a past relationship with the rapist or had you been hitchhiking when you were attacked?

Remember, too, that the defense attorney may employ techniques outside of the courtroom aimed at saving the rapist from conviction. These may include stalling tactics intended to drag the legal process out for so long that you become exhausted and angry, thereby hurting your ability to be a good witness for the state. The defense attorney may even contact you in an attempt to convince you to change your mind about continuing with the prosecution. A common technique is to try to make you feel unsure of the details or try to make you feel guilty for causing the rapist and his family so much trouble. If this happens, contact your prosecuting attorney immediately. You do not have to communicate with the defense attorney privately under any circumstances.

Step Four: The Preliminary Hearing

Shortly after the initial appearance (usually within one month), a preliminary hearing may be held. This hearing is becoming less common in criminal cases, but it is still a possibility. The preliminary hearing is quite similar to the initial appearance. Again, the suspect is informed of the charges against him and of his right to legal counsel. There is no determination of guilt or innocence.

There are critical differences between the preliminary hearing and the initial appearance, however. The most important of these differences is that you usually are required to attend the preliminary hearing. This can almost be thought of as a mini-trial. Here you will receive your first lesson in testifying before a court of law. The hearing will be brief, but you will be asked to tell the events of the rape before a magistrate, the prosecuting and defense attorneys and the rapist. You might be briefly cross-examined by the defense attorney. Finally, the magistrate will determine once again whether or not your case should be pursued further.

The preliminary hearing may seem unnecessary to you in light of all of the other legal procedures you face. The main reason for such a hearing, however, is that it offers the defense attorney an opportunity to become familiar with the extent of the evidence against his or her client (your rapist).

Remember, you are entitled to certain rights at each and every stage of the legal process. The preliminary hearing is no exception. For example, you have the right to request that the preliminary hearing be held in a closed courtroom. At the very least, you may be able to request that there be no media coverage for this or any other phase of the activities. You may even request that your name and address be withheld if you fear reprisal by the rapist should he learn who you are or where you live.

Step Five: An Information or Indictment

The next stage of the legal proceedings requires the prosecuting attorney to make a formal plea for court action to determine the guilt or innocence of the suspect. The formal request (complaint) can lead to either an indictment or an information.[1]

In the case of the indictment, the prosecutor files a complaint calling for action by a grand jury. A grand jury is made up of individuals who hear the details of the case. They do not decide guilt or innocence. Rather, they simply decide whether or not there is enough evidence to proceed with the case. If they feel there is, an indictment (sometimes called a "true bill") is issued. If they do not feel further proceedings are justified, they will order "no bill" and release the suspect. Therefore, the grand jury's perception of the case is very important. If they choose to indict, the suspect (defendant) is then bound over to a criminal court. At this point you are very close to an actual trial.

An information is similar to an indictment except that it by-passes the grand jury. A complaint is simply filed with a magistrate who again determines if the case should be pursued as is, if it should continue but with reduced charges or if the case should be dropped altogether.

---

[1]Step five differs dramatically from one area to another, even from case to case. For example, you may be asked to be present at a grand jury, but may not have to appear when an information is filed. Moreover, you may have to present testimony yourself, or the prosecuting attorney may simply read your signed statement. Be sure to ask the prosecutor what you might expect.

Step Six: The Arraignment

If the defendant is indicted, or if an information is filed against him, another formal hearing will follow. This is called the arraignment and is the time when the defendant enters a plea of guilty, not guilty or *nolo contendere* (meaning the defendant is not contesting the charges and can be sentenced to some form of punishment).

The defense attorney will probably suggest that the rapist "plea bargain," or plead guilty to a charge rather than plead innocent. This is a common tactic and one over which you have little or no control. Plea bargaining may be a relief to you in that it means you will not have to face a courtroom trial. The rapist will have already pleaded guilty and been sentenced. There are many reasons why your rapist would agree to plead guilty. One common reason is that the rapist is told if he is willing to plead guilty, his charges will be reduced. For example, a charge of rape could be reduced to a charge of assault and battery. Or, perhaps he is told he will receive a lighter sentence or a more lenient judge if he pleads guilty. For the crime of rape, the practice of plea bargaining has many advantages. It means the attorneys and the court system will need to spend less time processing your case. Most importantly, it means you will not have to appear before a trial jury to present the facts of your rape.

On the other hand, the practice can be frustrating as you watch your attacker plead guilty to a lesser charge and thereby receive a lighter sentence. The practice is not only very common for the crime of rape, it is also common for all other kinds of crimes. Be prepared for the possibility of plea bargaining in your case.

Step Seven: The Pre-Trial Conference

If your attacker pleads innocent at his arraignment, the next stage of the process which may occur (although it is not mandatory) is called a "pre-trial conference." One primary function of the conference is to inform you of the upcoming trial date and of the details of the trial itself.

Another function of the conference is to allow an opportunity for pre-trial motions to be heard. Pre-trial motions are introduced by the attorneys. They represent a request for evidence to be suppressed if it is believed such evidence was obtained illegally. Moreover, the defense attorney might request that the case be dropped due to a lack of sufficient evidence to convict the defendant. You may not have to be present when such motions are brought to conference.

Another kind of motion which affects you directly has to do with your own credibility. The defense attorney might request that you submit to a lie detector test or a psychiatric evaluation of your emotional state. Certainly the defense wants to prove that you are too "unbalanced" or "untruthful" to be believed. Remember, this is a normal tactic on the part of the defense and has nothing to do with your character *per se*. However, also remember that even truthful victims sometimes "fail" lie detector tests and psychiatric evaluations. Ask your prosecutor the following questions:

- Can you be forced to submit to such tests?

- How will the findings be used in court proceedings?

- If you can refuse the tests, does your refusal diminish your chances for receiving compensation[1] for the rape?

Proceed very cautiously with such requests.

_____

[1]Rape compensation is discussed later in this chapter.

Step Eight: The Trial

An actual courtroom trial is probably the best known step in the criminal justice system. Due to an increase in the use of plea bargaining, however, courtroom trials are becoming more and more rare in the prosecution of rape. Still, we tend to think of a trial as the final criminal justice procedure. Here the accused meets his accuser and is found guilty or innocent by an impartial body of jurors. If he is found guilty, he is sentenced and begins to pay his debt to society.

If your case ends in a trial (in other words, your attacker pleads not guilty to the charges against him), you should expect to wait as many as twelve months before actually going to court. You may be relieved to hear you will not have to go to trial before you have had time to begin your emotional recovery. However, the delay can also be frustrating in that you want to try to forget about the attack as quickly as possible. Feel free to stay in contact with the prosecuting attorney throughout the wait if you have any questions or concerns. Do not hesitate to contact the attorney if you are being harrassed or threatened in any way by the rapist, his attorney, his family or his friends.

Although we are familiar with courtroom scenes from the movies and television, few people have had much actual experience in a trial court. If you have never been to a trial, you may want to attend one while waiting for your own court date. It sometimes helps to become familiar with the courtroom itself and the activities of the various participants. Brush up on your legal terminology with a trained advocate or friend so that you will understand what is being discussed when you arrive in court.[1]

The trial will probably follow a standard format. Both the prosecutor and the defense attorney will call witnesses and present

---

[1]The glossary presented in Appendix C will be of help in your efforts to become familiar with legal terms.

evidence in order to build their cases. You will be asked to recount the events of the rape to the jury. After the attorneys have summarized their cases, the jury will decide upon a verdict. All of this can take anywhere from a few hours to several weeks. During much of that time you may be asked to wait in a private room adjacent to the courtroom, whether or not your presence is required in court that particular day. It can be very frustrating to wait day after day without being called. Be prepared for this possibility. You might want to ask a friend to accompany you if that would help pass the time.

One common exception to the standard courtroom proceedings should be mentioned. The defendant may have the right to request a non-jury trial, often called a "bench trial." The proceedings of the bench trial are quite similar to those of a jury trial. The only real difference is that a judge decides guilt or innocence rather than a body of jurors.

The most important role you will play in the trial is that of telling your story to the judge and/or jury. Be sure to present the facts of the rape clearly and confidently. You should rehearse your presentation beforehand. Reread the police report to be sure that all the information you provided to legal authorities is fresh in your mind. Again, writing or taping the presentation will help to avoid the pitfalls of contradicting yourself or seeming unsure of the facts.

Although the facts of the rape *should* speak for themselves, the truth is the *presentation* of the facts often sways the jury one way or another. Your demeanor or conduct on the witness stand will have a bearing on how you are perceived by the jury. Victims who dress in jeans and a t-shirt, or use foul language, are less likely to be taken seriously by a jury. Practice your presentation with "respectable" terms such as sodomy, fellatio, intercourse and ejaculation, as opposed to slang terms.[1] Your presentation

---

[1]Several appropriate terms and their definitions are included in the glossary at the end of this book.

should be clear, understandable and concise. If it helps to have a friendly and supportive face in the room with you, ask a spouse, friend or advocate to accompany you to court.

You will also be questioned by the rapist's attorney in front of the jurors. Remember, his or her job is to discredit you. A variety of techniques might be used to accomplish this. The defense attorney might try to confuse you by asking complicated or irrelevant questions. Or, she or he may focus on miniscule details of the attack in an effort to force you to contradict yourself on some minor fact. The defense attorney might even imply you encouraged the attack by exhibiting enticing behavior or by using poor judgment.

These techniques can result in the attorney asking misleading or accusatory questions. Be prepared to answer such questions as straight-forwardly as you possibly can. Sometimes victims are required to supply only "yes" or "no" answers. However, you will usually be able to say as much as you feel is necessary. Use this opportunity to your advantage. If, for example, you are asked, "Did you encourage the accused by manually stimulating an erection?" you could answer, "He forced me to touch his genitals."

Another court issue relates to your past history. Several areas have limited the extent to which the defense attorney can introduce evidence meant to make you appear promiscuous. "Shield laws" have been enacted which protect the privacy of victims. Under such laws, your sexual history is inadmissible in court. Other areas still allow the details of your sexual past as evidence, often accompanied by a "cautionary charge" to the jury, made by the judge, that this evidence should not be used to influence the jury's decision. This is a very controversial issue, especially in light of the fact that the rapist's sexual history is not admissible in court. Be sure to talk to the prosecuting attorney about this issue *before* you go to court. Ask about shield laws in your area. To what extent can evidence against you be introduced? Can evidence pertaining to any prior sexual relationship be introduced? Or, can your sexuality be brought up only if another man's semen, in addition to that of the rapist's, was found in the medical examination? Tell the prosecutor everything that is important for him or her to know in order to prepare in advance for witnesses or evidence which the defense attorney might introduce. Suggest character witnesses who can testify on your behalf. This may seem offensive and unnecessary, but until every area changes its laws to exclude the victim's character from the trial it is important for you to be prepared.

In many cases, your legal responsibilities come to a close when the trial ends. One exception to this would be if the rapist is found guilty and chooses to appeal the conviction (take his case to a higher court). If this happens, you may again be called as a witness. Ask the prosecuting attorney about this possibility early on so that you can be prepared.

Step Nine: Sentencing

The final stage in the prosecution process (barring an appeal) is the sentencing of the rapist. Men who plead guilty to charges, or who are found guilty by a judge or jury, are sentenced to some form of punishment. Hopefully, the punishment your rapist receives will be satisfactory in your mind and you will feel the rapist "got what he deserved" for what he did to you. Although his punishment can never undo the crime committed against you, it may make you feel safer and better about yourself to know that he, too, is paying for the crime.

There is no guarantee, however, that you will find a sense of satisfaction from the sentence. Your rapist may be sentenced to a short prison term. He may not go to prison at all, but rather be ordered to serve a probationary sentence. The court may insist he receive psychiatric counseling with the thought that this will "correct" his aberrant behavior in the future. The judge who orders punishment for your rapist will have a variety of sentencing options. It is important for you to be prepared for a possible disappointment at this final stage of the process.

Some rape victims even report that they feel a temporary sense of guilt or remorse at this time, regardless of the sentence handed down. They feel responsible for having put the rapist and his family through a difficult ordeal. If you are raped, remember that it is not unusual to feel sensitive to the needs of these other people. However also remember that you were seriously wronged by the rapist. He had no right to do what he did and should be punished for his crime. Be assured that these guilt feelings will pass in time.

The Benefits of Prosecution

The above discussion makes clear the actual steps of rape prosecution. Prosecution procedures are never easy. Victims have to tell their story often, they may fear retaliation and they may lose the conviction. If you are raped, ask yourself how this will make you feel about your own emotional well-being, as well as your safety.

On the other hand, the benefits of prosecution are many. The process of objectively stating the facts concerning the rape may make you feel less anxious and distraught. It affords you the opportunity to ventilate or release your anger and pain. Now you are in charge, rather than the rapist. Research has shown that women who prosecute often recover from rape more quickly. It is thought that being seen as "The Victim" by others helps you to stop blaming yourself. You may also feel a sense of pride in having protected other would-be victims from this man.

Moreover, the benefits of prosecution have increased as attitudes about the crime of rape change. Victims' rights are being recognized and protected more today than before. For example, many areas now recognize victims by providing financial compensation directly to victims, regardless of whether or not the rapist is convicted. A victim simply petitions to a compensation board for funds to cover medical expenses, loss of income and any other financial losses incurred as a result of the rape. Your rape crisis center or prosecuting attorney will be able to inform you of such programs. Be sure to ask about the availability of compensation in your area.

Another alternative is to bring civil charges against your attacker. This can be done whether or not a criminal prosecution is underway. It is important to recognize that there are differences between a civil and a criminal proceeding. In a civil suit, you hire a lawyer to represent you and file a complaint against the rapist. You are no longer a witness, but rather a plaintiff (the one making the complaint). In this case, you may not be required to tell your story in court unless the defense attorney calls upon you and asks you to do so. The lawyer for the defense is less likely to ask you to tell your story in full, rather she or he will ask only those questions which help the defendant and/or diminish your credibility. Often, your own attorney will anticipate these questions and coach you beforehand.

Another difference between a criminal and a civil proceeding is that a judgment can be made in your favor even if there is reasonable doubt (in the eyes of the law, of course) about the guilt of your attacker. Unlike a criminal court, a civil court requires only a "preponderance of evidence" to determine guilt. Criminal courts insist that guilt be proven "beyond all reasonable doubt." This is an important difference. It means you can win your case even though some uncertainty about the rapist's guilt still exists. The evidence does not have to be air-tight, but only complete enough to convince a judge that there is a good chance this person raped you.

If a judgment is given in your favor (in other words, you win your case) you may receive a monetary award for physical and/or psychological impairment, loss of income, medical and rehabilitation costs, the cost of your lawyer and the like. There are other positive aspects to bringing a civil suit. As an individual bringing charges against someone who severely wronged you, you may feel less like a cog in the legal machine. You might instead feel like a person who is regaining control over her life. Being able to avenge your violation in this way provides a useful outlet for pent-up anger and frustration.

In addition to bringing civil charges against your attacker, you may be able to file charges against any person or institution that played a significant role in your being attacked. These include towns, businesses or governments that neglected to provide responsible measures for your safety. For instance, if you were attacked in an improperly lighted parking area, you can bring civil charges against the owner of the facility.

Finally, if your personal property is damaged or stolen by the rapist, the loss of property may be deductible from your taxes. For example, you can deduct losses if your home or apartment was vandalized, your jewelry stolen or your clothing destroyed by the rapist. Contact the Internal Revenue Service for further information.

For Your Consideration

Whether you are involved in the legal process as a witness in a criminal case or a plaintiff with civil charges, there are some additional points you should keep in mind:

- If at any time you receive threats from your attacker or his associates, you should report this to the authorities immediately. This not only helps to ensure your personal safety, but also increases your credibility as a witness in a criminal proceeding and helps to reinforce your claims in a civil suit. In some areas, you will be able to obtain an order from the court (a restraining order) which prevents the attacker from contacting you in any way. Call the police immediately if you are threatened by the attacker.

- Whenever you are asked to give testimony in court, how you appear and how you speak will make an impression upon the judge and jury. Dressing conservatively and speaking with confidence and sincerity are very important. If you are uncertain about any of these things, ask for the help and advice of your prosecuting attorney, personal lawyer or advocate. They may suggest that you curtail some of your normal activities until the trial is over. Do not take these suggestions as an insult. You must remember that your attacker's lawyer will be looking for any opportunity to lower your credibility as a witness or plaintiff.

- If at any time during the process you do not understand any legal procedures, feel free to ask questions of your prosecuting attorney or lawyer. The legal process is often a long and trying affair. However, there is absolutely no reason for you to be treated poorly. If you are not getting proper treatment, complain to the appropriate authorities.

- Check into victim support services, such as emotional counseling and legal advice, offered in your area. The prosecuting attorney's office can provide you with such information.

- You may wish to examine rape laws and civil codes in order to determine if your case is being handled properly. This can often be a therapeutic activity helping you to regain control of your own life. Ask your reference librarian for the appropriate materials.

Improving Rape Laws

There is a tremendous amount of variation in rape laws from one region to the next. This variation reflects the current diversity of attitudes concerning the crime of rape. As such, there is debate concerning what form future laws should take. Some localities have taken positive steps to revamp rape laws, making them more responsive to the needs of victims and increasing the conviction rate of accused rapists. Michigan, Minnesota and California are some of the states which have devised enlightened rape laws designed to achieve these goals. For example, in Minnesota, the rape victim no longer has to prove the rape was actively resisted. Another provision of the Minnesota statutes requires the county to pay for the medical evidence gathering and post-rape treatment of victims. Many municipalities have set up special rape police and prosecution units which are more effective in prosecuting and convicting rapists.

Despite these encouraging examples, many areas retain backward legal attitudes. As a result, a number of changes have been suggested. These include:

- Making laws sexually neutral; that is, removing any consideration of the sex of the victim or of the rapist

- No longer making it necessary to prove that the victim attempted to resist, that vaginal penetration occurred or that the crime can be corroborated by a third person

- Preventing introduction of the victim's prior sexual conduct

- Increasing the opportunities for prosecuting husband and acquaintance rapes

- Changing rape from an all-or-nothing proposition to rape by degrees. The severity of the rape would determine the degree of penalty for the accused. This change might make convictions easier to obtain.

Wishful thinking alone will not bring about these needed changes in rape laws. Professionals and lay persons alike must become involved to change attitudes and laws regarding rape. We must also work together to prevent rape from happening in the first place. The need for and benefits of such involvement will be discussed in the next chapter.

11

Becoming Involved

Now is the time to ask what can be done to help prevent rape. We must also ask what can be done to help lessen its impact upon individual victims and upon society in general. The answer is for individuals to work toward an elimination of the burden of rape. In this chapter we will discuss how *you* can get involved to fight against the crime of rape.

Why Become Involved?

There are a number of reasons why individual involvement in the prevention of rape is important. First, it has been shown that when people get involved, the conditions for rape victims improve. For example, many people have fought to rewrite rape laws. When laws are changed for the better, the number of successful prosecutions of rapists increases, which decreases the likelihood that each individual rapist will make others his victims. Moreover, when laws change the general treatment and recovery of victims improve. This is true today in a number of areas world-wide. This one example helps to illustrate the point that when constructive action is taken, the crime of rape can be successfully combatted and the services to victims improved.

There may be other, more personal reasons for joining the fight against rape. If you have been a victim of rape, getting involved in the fight against rape may mean an improved sense of control over your life and a greater sense of self-worth. For those who have not been raped, helping to fight rape is the best way to relieve the fear, anger and frustration that come with knowing that rape is a part of our society. Many people have found this to be true as they work to open and maintain the over 700 rape crisis centers across the United States. Such centers have led to a dramatic improvement in rape victim care. Staffed by women and men dedicated to decreasing the occurrence of rape and its impact upon victims, these centers provide a number of essential services. Counseling for the victim and her family, legal and medical advocacy, 24-hour crisis telephone lines, short-term child care and community education are just some of the services offered by these centers. Some also have short-term financial aid as well as victim job and home relocation programs. These organizations serve as prime examples of what can be done to help rape victims.

How To Become Involved

The question becomes, "What can I do to become involved in the fight against rape?" Listed below are just a few suggestions you might consider.

- Join in an effort to establish, operate or expand the services of a rape crisis center in your area. The benefits of these centers to rape victims have already been detailed.

- Work to change the laws. This can be at the local or national level. Petition drives, voter registration drives and other political actions are needed to change existing rape laws so that they are more responsive to the needs of victims, more effective in the deterrence of rape and more efficient in the arrest and conviction of rapists.

- Become an active member or participate in organizations such as the National Organization for Women (NOW) or Women

Against Pornography. It is widely believed that one of the fundamental reasons rape occurs in our culture is that women have been viewed traditionally as objects of male domination and control. NOW and other organizations are committed to changing this condition. Your involvement in their work may help in this cause.

- Become active in groups that put pressure on governmental, law enforcement, judicial and health care officials to make them more aware of and sensitive to the crime of rape as well as the needs of victims. Ask that these officials work to improve public safety, promote rape victim care, include rape with anti-crime programs and set up special rape crisis law enforcement, prosecution and victim health care teams.

- Become active in neighborhood organizations. Most of these organizations are concerned with the deterrence of crime. As a member of one of these groups, you can be instrumental in ensuring that the crime of rape is not overlooked.

- You might become involved in the study of rape. A vast amount of work needs to be done in this area if we are ever to understand its causes, consequences and prevention.

- Check into what measures are being taken against rape at your place of employment. Rape on or near the work place is a major contributor to the high number of rapes that occur. Encourage your union to make employee security an issue in contract negotiations. If you are not represented by a union, you may wish to check with your supervisor as to what can be done. This may be a difficult step to take, but often if you proceed thoughtfully, and if this is an issue that concerns many of your co-workers, management will be responsive.

- If you are a student or teacher, become involved in a campus rape crisis center or organization devoted to fighting rape.

- Help to organize community programs designed to promote awareness of the crime of rape. This can often be accomplished by setting up workshops, presentations and rape programs in schools, clubs, churches, synagogues and other community organizations. Perhaps you could help to publish and distribute a document outlining all of the specific laws as well as medical and legal procedures relative to rape in your area.

Law enforcement, governmental, judicial and health-care professionals hold a special place of responsibility in our society. If you count yourself among one of these groups, getting actively involved against the crime of rape should be of particular significance to you. Some of the above suggestions may be of value if you decide to take positive action against rape. You may be able to do a great deal to affect worthwhile change simply by virtue of your position. The following suggestions are presented for your consideration:

- Keep an open mind toward community input concerning rape. Carefully consider suggestions for improving public safety, law enforcement and health care. Respond to them in a way that encourages members of your community to stay involved. To serve the public trust, take the time to become more informed about the problems and possible solutions to rape in your area.

- Help to sponsor, organize and attend professional seminars and workshops that deal with the subject of rape.

- If you are a member of the legal, law enforcement or judicial profession you can help by making the local laws and statutes concerning rape available to local organizations dealing with rape victim treatment, rape prevention and rapist prosecution. Compile a pamphlet which spells out exactly what the laws are in your area.

- Organize rape crisis teams among your colleagues. These are important in emergency rooms, among police officers, investigators and prosecutors. Outline the specific procedures to be followed in the treatment of rape victims. Coordinate and extend all of the services offered through your organization to ensure that they are made fully available to each and every victim.

- Take the lead in establishing community education programs. Using your expertise, teach others what you know about rape prevention, treatment and prosecution. This might include school programs, presentations to organizations and other professionals, newspaper interviews and local radio and television messages.

- Volunteer your services to rape crisis centers. This will help to keep you in touch with the everyday workings of rape treatment organizations. You will also be in a position to counsel and advise such groups as to the rights and responsibilities of rape victims in your area.

- Try to set up rape victim teams which link together the services of doctors, nurses, police officers, counselors and other professionals. A team approach to assisting the rape victim is often the most helpful because it is coordinated and ensures that all the necessary services are provided. This means that services will not be duplicated, but it also means that some services will not be withheld simply because of a lack of communication.

- Speak out for legal reform in the area of rape. Several suggestions have been discussed in this book which would help in the prosecution and conviction of rapists. If your area is not in the forefront of legal reform, you may want to push for such changes.

The eradication of rape ultimately depends upon the efforts of citizens. Rape can only be successfully eliminated if individuals come together to confront and combat the crime.

12

A Final Word

Any person who has been raped has been through a terrible ordeal. If you are raped, no one can undo the tragedy. It is possible, however, that the ordeal can be made easier for you. This book was written to remind you that you are not alone. Many resources (emotional, medical and legal) exist today that were unheard of only a few years ago. These resources can and should be tapped, for they exist to serve you.

Remember also that you are your own most important resource. As other rape victims have reported, you too will find that your recovery from rape becomes easier and easier as time passes. It is important to remember this fact as you face the crime of rape. Try to remember the following whenever you think about your attack:

- You did not cause this crime in any way, shape or form. Your actions are totally separate from the violence to be found in some men.

- You reacted to the crime in the way that made the most sense to you at the time. Do not rely on ''hindsight'' to evaluate what you did or said.

- Your emotional responses after the rape are natural for you. Be kind to yourself and allow yourself the time *you* need to recover.

- Take whatever steps you need to adjust to the rape. Resume your normal routine as much as possible. Talk to your partner, family, friends, an advocate or a counselor about your feelings as much as you find helpful.

- Medical and legal help are available to you. Use these services, and remember to ask questions to make sure that the care you receive is the very best possible.

Most importantly, remember that you are still in charge of your own life. *There is no way to excuse the crime of rape, but you can recover from it.*

Appendix A
Resources

To find the number of your local rape crisis center:

• Check the telephone directory.

• Call your local hospital or police department.

• Call other human service agencies you are aware of in your area such as United Way, the YWCA, Protective Services or other mental health agencies.

• Contact one of the national centers listed below for information about your own community.

> National Center for the Prevention and Control of Rape
> Room 6C-12, Parklawn Building
> 5600 Fishers Lane
> Rockville, MD 20857
> (301) 443-1910   new # 443 3728

> National Coalition Against Sexual Assault (NCASA)*
> P.O. Box 7156
> Austin, TX 78712
> (512) 472-7273

*At the time of this printing, NCASA is working toward having a national office. However, it currently establishes its headquarters on a rotating basis with the individual serving a two-year term as its president. The Austin Rape Crisis Center has kindly allowed us to list that agency where the current president is located and will provide the correct NCASA address and phone number as it changes in the future.

Be Prepared

The best way to be prepared for the crime of rape is to know in advance whom to call, what to do and what to expect. Such preparation will mean that if you are raped, you will not have to hunt for phone numbers and face totally unfamiliar situations. The information provided in this appendix will help you to be prepared. Moreover, it will help you to make decisions *in advance* regarding what to do in the event that you are raped. You will be able to choose the best services in your area. You will have a handy reference for the names and phone numbers of those to whom you can turn in an emergency. This information will be tremendously comforting to you, if you are raped.

A.   Rape Crisis Centers:

Some areas have several rape crisis centers while others, unfortunately, have none. Find out what is available in your area. If you are in a position to choose from among several centers, base your decision on the number and extent of services each provides:

1.   Are medical and legal advocacy provided? That is, do crisis center volunteers accompany a victim throughout the post-rape process to support her and remind her of her rights?

2.   Are counseling services available?

3.   Does the rape crisis center provide temporary child care?

4.   Is a shelter available where a victim might stay for a few days immediately following the rape?

5. Will crisis center volunteers meet a victim at the hospital and bring her a change of clothes?

6. Does the center provide any short-term, emergency financial support for victims?

7. Other

_____

_____

(Note the name and the phone number of the rape crisis center in the section provided at the end of this appendix.)

B. Medical Care:

If you are raped, it is vitally important that you receive prompt and thorough medical attention. This poses problems for some rape victims. Some go to a hospital which does not provide adequate care. Others go to a hospital which does not work diligently to protect victims' rights. Still others fail to seek medical care due to financial concerns. It is to your advantage to make some phone calls immediately to find out which area hospitals provide the most care. The following "checklist" will help you to choose a facility in your area best suited to rape victim care:

1. A great many medical facilities exist to serve the victims of rape. You may want to call a hospital emergency room, a medical clinic or even your personal physician. Choose any of these potential medical facilities, depending on which is the most cooperative and thorough.

2. Ask each facility to outline the standard procedures taken in the treatment of rape victims.

3. Ask representatives of each facility what special services are offered to rape victims. For example, a private

waiting room for victims; a policy which allows friends or advocates to accompany victims throughout the medical process; an interpreter for non-English speaking victims?

4. Does the facility have its own ambulance service with a crew trained in rape crisis techniques?

5. Are counseling services available through the medical facility?

6. What is the nature of the relationship between the medical facility and the legal authorities? For example: Does the medical facility have a special evidence collection kit and, if so, what does it entail? Do the medical authorities automatically call the police when a rape victim seeks care, or is this the victim's right? Does the facility automatically test for drugs or alcohol in the victim's bloodstream? Does the facility notify the media in any way? Are separate forms used to catalog personal information which has nothing to do with the crime of rape? Does all medical evidence have to be released to the police by the victim and, if so, what is the nature of the release procedure (for example, a signed form or simple verbal agreement)?

7. What forms of follow-up care are provided by the facility?

8. Are victims notified of their need for pregnancy and venereal disease tests several weeks after the attack?

9. What financial arrangements can be made through the facility to cover the expenses of rape victim care?

10.   Other

_____

_____

Once you have decided upon a medical facility, note the phone number in the space provided below. Do not forget to include the number of the ambulance service, if different from the facility itself. Some areas now have a two or three digit phone number to be dialed in all types of emergencies. You may want to note the emergency phone number in your area. Ask for the ambulance/medical facility of your choosing should you ever have to dial this number.

C.   Legal Procedures:

As has been said, the more you know about the specific legal procedures in your area, the better your position to prosecute successfully. Take the time to get some answers to the following questions. Call your local police department, prosecuting attorney or private lawyer for the information you need:

1.   Does your local police department have a special rape crisis unit?

2.   Are female officers available?

3.   Do police officers who respond to the initial call for help write down the victim's testimony verbatim, or do they only take notes in their own words?

4.   What steps are taken by the police department to safeguard a victim from further attacks by the same man?

5.   What legally constitutes "rape" in your area? Does rape only include vaginal intercourse? What about husband-

wife rape? Must a victim prove that she resisted force? Are witnesses necessary to corroborate a charge of rape?

6. Is courtroom testimony allowed which might damage the character of victims? Many areas have placed restrictions (commonly referred to as "Shield Laws") on such testimony. Find out whether you have a Shield Law in your area and, if so, the nature and extent of protection it provides.

7. Does your local prosecuting attorney's office have a special rape crisis unit? Do they provide para-professional advocates or other victims' support services to work on the victims' behalf?

8. How often are victims forced to cooperate with the prosecutor as subpoenaed witnesses? To what extent can a victim "change her mind" and decide not to prosecute?

9. Can a victim refuse to take polygraph tests or be subjected to blood analyses? Can such refusal be admitted to a court of law?

10. Is a victim allowed her own attorney to oversee the prosecution? Can the attorney press civil charges against the rapist?

11. What are the exact steps in the criminal justice process? What sentencing practices are common for the crime of rape? Is plea bargaining a common practice in your area?

12. Does your area have a restitution program to compensate for financial loss due to rape? If so, how does a victim qualify for support? Are there any stipulations

which must be met in order to qualify (for example, cooperation with the prosecuting attorney, prompt reporting of the crime to the police, a minimal dollar amount of damages and so forth)?

13.   Other

_____

_____

D.   Friends and Family:

If you are raped, the people who are important to you will be instrumental in your recovery. Take some time now to talk to them about the crime of rape. Open the communication lines immediately. The following suggestions will help in this area:

1.   Find friends who share your concerns about rape. Talk about how you feel about the crime. Exchange phone numbers so that you can be there for each other immediately, in case of emergency.

2.   As you communicate about rape, find out what myths, if any, are still believed by your friends and family. Suggest to them that such myths are erroneous and dangerous. You might want to share a copy of this book with them.

3.   Suggest that you and the people you love get involved in the fight against rape. Working together can form a permanent bond between people that is very important in case of rape.

4.   Other

_____

_____

E.   Phone Numbers:

Write down the names and telephone numbers of important people and services below:

Local Name	Contact Person	Phone Number
Rape Crisis Center		
_____	_____	_____
_____	_____	_____
Police Department		
_____	_____	_____
_____	_____	_____
Rape Task Unit of the Police Department		
_____	_____	ext.: _____
_____	_____	ext.: _____
Private Attorney (if applicable)		
_____	_____	_____
_____	_____	_____
Hospital or Other Medical Facility with Rape Care		
_____	_____	_____
_____	_____	_____
Prosecuting Attorney		
_____	_____	_____
_____	_____	_____
Ambulance Service		
_____	_____	_____
_____	_____	_____
Personal Physician (if applicable)		
_____	_____	_____
_____	_____	_____
Counseling Services		
_____	_____	_____
_____	_____	_____
Other		
_____	_____	_____
_____	_____	_____

F.   If You Are Raped:

If you are raped, you will no doubt encounter a great many professionals as you seek help. It is very easy for the names and faces of these people to blend together, making it difficult to remember whom to contact with follow-up questions and concerns. If you are raped, always note the names of the people with whom you come into contact in the space provided.

Name/Badge Number and Other identification.	Position (for example nurse, police investigator...)	Telephone Number
Rape Advocate(s)		
_____	_____	_____
_____	_____	_____
Medical Staff		
_____	_____	_____
_____	_____	_____
Police Officers		
_____	_____	_____
_____	_____	_____
Prosecutor's Office		
_____	_____	_____
_____	_____	_____
Other		
_____	_____	_____
_____	_____	_____

Appendix C
Glossary

If you are raped, and especially if you choose to prosecute, you may hear a great many words and phrases with which you are unfamiliar. It is to your advantage to understand such terms, to be able to use them yourself and to incorporate them into your testimony. The following glossary should be helpful in this effort. However, it cannot be emphasized strongly enough that you should feel free to ask questions about anything you do not understand.

Accused — Another name for the defendant, the person charged with a crime. (Also referred to as the suspect or alleged perpetrator.)

Adjudication — To settle a case in court.

Alleged — Suspected, but still without proof.

Anal intercourse — Sexual penetration of the anus.

Appeal — The transfer of a case from a lower court to a higher court for a new hearing.

Arraignment — Bring a defendant into court to answer charges brought against him or her.

Bail — Usually money, given as a guarantee to court officials that a suspect will appear for trial.

Beyond a reasonable doubt — In a criminal court, the prosecution must prove the defendant's guilt beyond all reasonable doubt.

Cervix — The outer end of the uterus.

Civil law — Law dealing with the rights of private citizens.

Clitoris — A female, external sex organ.

Coitus — Sexual intercourse.

Condom — Thin rubber protective device used to cover the penis during intercourse which prevents fertilization and disease transmission.

Consent — Voluntary and willing agreement.

Conviction — Finding someone guilty of a crime.

Corroboration — Other evidence used to prove the truth of a statement, anything that substantiates or further proves other evidence.

Criminal attempt — To prepare for, plan and try to commit a crime.

Criminal law — Law dealing with criminal behavior.

Cunnilingus — Oral stimulation of the clitoris or entire vulva.

Defendant — The person against whom civil or criminal action is brought, the person accused of the crime.

Defense — The defendant's arguments and evidence of innocence.

Defense attorney — The attorney representing the defendant, may be called defense counsel.

Discretion — The freedom to act or judge on one's own, without legal rulings.

Disposition — The final settlement of a case.

District attorney — The prosecuting lawyer, representing the state.

Ejaculation — The discharge of semen from the penis.

Erection — An enlarged and hardened penis.

Evidence — Any statements and objects presented to a court as proof.

Exhibitionism — Exposing one's sex organs to the public.

Fellatio — Oral stimulation of the penis.

Felony — A serious crime.

Fornication — Sexual intercourse between people not married to each other.

Genitals (genitalia) — The sex organs.

Grand jury — A group of people who evaluate the evidence against a suspect to decide whether or not to indict, or send to trial.

Hymen — The tissue which may cover the vaginal opening.

Indictment — An accusation by a grand jury that a suspect should be tried for a crime. If a judge makes this decision instead of a grand jury, it is said that an "information is filed."

Insemination — When semen is introduced into the vagina.

Magistrate — A lower court judge.

Misdemeanor — A minor crime.

Orgasm — Sexual climax for either sex.

Parole — Being allowed to leave prison earlier than the original sentence stated as long as rules and regulations are followed.

Phallic object — Any object resembling a penis in shape which might be used against a victim sexually.

Plaintiff — The person who brings a lawsuit against someone else.

Plea bargaining — The prosecutor and the accused make a deal in the case. Usually, the deal that is made requires the accused to plead guilty to a lesser offense, or to plead guilty and receive a lighter sentence.

Polygraph — A lie detector machine.

Preliminary hearing — An early proceeding to determine whether there is a good chance that a particular person committed a crime.

Preponderance of evidence — The amount of evidence required to prove guilt in a civil case; less evidence is needed than in a criminal case where it is necessary to prove guilt beyond a reasonable doubt.

Probable cause — A good chance that a crime has been committed, enough cause to suspect a crime occurred. Probable cause needs to be proven before a case goes to trial.

Probation — A convicted criminal is allowed to stay out of prison altogether if certain rules and regulations are followed.

Prosecution — Legal, court action taken against a defendant to decide guilt or innocence.

Prosecutrix — A woman who charges a crime, such as rape, has been committed.

Public defender — An attorney provided free of charge to a defendant.

Recidivist — An habitual or repeating criminal.

Release on recognizance (ROR) — Sometimes used instead of bail, an accused is set free on the promise that he or she will appear in court to answer charges.

Restitution — The act of restoring something to its rightful owner, making good.

Scrotum — The outside sac of skin enclosing the testicles of males.

Semen — The sperm-carrying secretion from a penis.

Sexual assault — Physical, sexual advances against a person who does not consent, with or without actual intercourse.

Sodomy — Any sexual act which is defined by the state as "unnatural," (for example, between an adult and a child).

Spermatozoa — Sperm; the male reproductive cell carried in the semen, released from the penis during ejaculation.

Statutes — Legislative laws, laws enacted by a government.

Testicle — One of two male reproductive glands found in the scrotum.

Testimony — The evidence given under oath by a witness in court.

Tort — A wrong committed by one person against another, a civil wrong.

Unfounded — A case which has not yet been established as fact.

Vagina — In females, the canal leading from the external genitals to the uterus.

Venereal disease — Any one of several sexually transmitted diseases.

Vulva — All external female genitalia.

Appendix D
References

Amir, Menachem. *Patterns in Forcible Rape*. Chicago: The University of Chicago Press, 1971.

Bennet, James R. "A Model for Evaluation: Design for a Rape Counseling Program." *Child Welfare*, 61(6):395-400. June, 1977.

Bode, Janet. *Fighting Back: How to Cope with the Medical, Emotional, and Legal Consequences of Rape*. New York: Macmillan Publishing Co., Inc., 1978.

Boulding, Elise. "Women and Social Violence." *International Social Science Journal*, 30(4):801-815. 1978.

Bowker, Lee (ed.), *Women and Crime in America*. New York: Macmillan Publishing Co., Inc., A Glencoe Book, 1981.

Braen, G. Richard. "Rape and Sexual Assault of the Adolescent and Adult Female." *Topics in Emergency Medicine*, 4(3):55-64. January, 1982.

Brownmiller, Susan. *Against Our Will: Men, Women and Rape*. New York: Simon and Schuster, 1975.

Burgess, Ann Wolbert and Holmstrom, Lynda Lytle. "Crisis and Counseling Requests of Rape Victims." *Nursing Research*, 23(3):196-202. May-June, 1974.

Burgess, Ann Wolbert and Holmstrom, Lynda Lytle. "Rape Trauma Syndrome." *American Journal of Psychiatry*, 131(9):981-986. September, 1974.

Burgess, Ann Wolbert and Holmstrom, Lynda Lytle. *Rape: Victims of Crisis*. Bowie, MD: Robert J. Brady Co., 1974.

Burgess, Ann Wolbert and Holmstrom, Lynda Lytle. "Coping Behavior of the Rape Victim." *American Journal of Psychiatry*, 133(4):413-418. 1976.

Burt, Martha R. "Cultural Myths and Supports for Rape." *Journal of Personality and Social Psychology*, 38(2):217-230. February, 1980.

Calhoun, Karen S., Atkeson, Beverly M. and Resick, Beverly M. "A Longitudinal Examination of Fear Reactions in Victims of Rape." *Journal of Counseling Psychology*, 29(6):655-661. November, 1982.

Chapman, Jane Roberts and Gates, Margaret (eds.), *The Victimization of Women*. Beverly Hills, CA: Sage Publications, 1978.

Chappell, Duncan, et al., (eds.), *Forcible Rape: The Crime, the Victim and the Offender*. New York: Columbia University Press, 1977.

Chicago Hospital Council in Cooperation with the Citizens Committee for Victim Assistance. *Guidelines for the Treatment of Victims of Suspected Sexual Assault*. Chicago: Chicago Hospital Council, 1981.

Connell, Noreen and Wilson, Cassandra. *Rape: The First Sourcebook for Women*. New York: New American Library, 1974.

Davis, Linda J. and Brody, Elaine M. *Rape and Older Women: A Guide to Prevention and Protection*. U.S. Department of Health, Education and Welfare, Public Health Service, National Institute of Mental Health, 1979.

DeCrow, Karen. *Sexist Justice*. New York: Vintage Books, 1974.

Denham, Priscilla, L. "Toward an Understanding of Child Rape." *Journal of Pastoral Care*, 36(4):235-245. December, 1982.

Dowd, Maureen. "Rape: The Sexual Weapon." *Time*, September 5, 1983.

Estabrook, Barbara, Fessenden, Ruth, Dumas, Mary and McBride, Thomas C. "Rape on Campus: Community Education and Services for Victims." *Journal of the American College Health Association*, 27(2):72-74. October, 1978.

Feild, Hubert S. "Attitudes Toward Rape: A Comparative Analysis of Police, Rapists, Crisis Counselors, and Citizens." *Journal of Personality and Social Psychology*, 36(2):156-179. February, 1978.

Finkelhor, David. *Sexually Victimized Children*. New York: The Free Press, 1979.

Foley, Theresa S. and Davies, Marilyn A. *Rape: Nursing Care of Victims*. St. Louis: The C.V. Mosby Co., 1983.

Gage, Robert W. "Program for Rape Victims Applauded." *Journal of the American College Health Association*, 27(2):67. October, 1978.

Griffin, Susan. *Rape: The Power of Consciousness*. San Francisco: Harper & Row, Publishers, 1979.

Groth, A. Nicholas. "Rape: Behavioral Aspects." In Sanford H. Kadish (ed.), *Encyclopedia of Crime and Justice*, Vol. 4. New York: The Free Press, 1983.

Groth, A. Nicholas and Burgess, Ann W. "Male Rape: Offenders and Victims." *American Journal of Psychiatry*, 137(7):806-810. July, 1980.

Hacker, Andrew (ed.), *U.S. A Statistical Portrait*. New York: Viking Press, 1983.

Hardgrove, Grace. "An Interagency Service Network to Meet Needs of Rape Victims." *Social Casework*, 57(4):245-253. April, 1976.

Harris, Lucy Reed. "Towards a Consent Standard in the Law of Rape." *University of Chicago Law Review*, 43(3):613-645. 1976.

Harris, Marvin. "Why Men Dominate Women." *The New York Times Magazine Section*, 13:46. November, 1977.

Hilberman, Elaine. "Rape: The Ultimate Violation of Self." *American Journal of Psychiatry*, 133(4):436-437. April, 1976.

Hoff, Lee Ann and Williams, Tim. "Counseling the Rape Victim and Her Family." *Crisis Intervention*, 6(4):2-13. 1975.

Katz, Sedelle and Mazur, Mary Ann. *Understanding the Rape Victim: A Synthesis of Research Findings*. New York: John Wiley & Sons, 1979.

Kilpatrick, Dean G., Veronen, Lois J. and Resick, Patricia A. "The Aftermath of Rape: Recent Empirical Findings." *American Journal of Orthopsychiatry*, 49(4):658-669. October, 1979.

Krulewitz, Judith E. "Reactions to Rape Victims: Effects of Rape Circumstances, Victim's Emotional Response, and Sex of Helper." *Journal of Counseling Psychology*, 29(6):645-654. November, 1982.

Macdonald, John M. *Rape: Offenders and Their Victims*. Springfield, IL: Charles C. Thomas, Publisher, 1971.

McCahill, Thomas W., Meyer, Linda C. and Fischman, Arthur M. *The Aftermath of Rape*. Lexington, MA: Lexington Books, 1979.

McCombie, Sharon L., Bassuk, Ellen, Savitz, Roberta and Pell, Susan. "Development of a Medical Center—Rape Crisis Intervention Program." *American Journal of Psychiatry*, 133(4):418-421. April, 1976.

Meiners, Roger E. *Victim Compensation: Economic, Legal, and Political Aspects*. Lexington, MA: Lexington Books, 1978.

Mills, Patrick and Sachs, Lee (eds.), *Rape Intervention and Resource Manual*. Springfield, IL: Charles C. Thomas, Publisher, 1977.

Norris, Jeanette and Feldman-Summers, Shirley. "Factors Related to the Psychological Impacts of Rape on the Victim." *Journal of Abnormal Psychology*, 90(6):562-567. December, 1981.

Notman, Malkah T., and Nadelson, Carol C. "The Rape Victim: Psychodynamic Considerations." *American Journal of Psychiatry*, 133(4):408-413. April, 1976.

Rada, Richard T. (ed.), *Clinical Aspects of the Rapist*. New York: Grune & Stratton, 1978.

Reid, Sue Titus. *Crime and Criminology*. 3rd edition, New York: Holt, Rinehart and Winston, 1982.

Richardson, Laurel Walum. *The Dynamics of Sex and Gender: A Sociological Perspective*. Boston: Houghton Mifflin Co., 1981.

Robinson, G. Erlick. "Management of the Rape Victim." *Canadian Medical Association Journal*, 15(6):520-522. September 18, 1976.

Rodkin, Lawrence I., Hunt, E. Joan and Cowan, Suzi Dunstan. "A Men's Support Group for Significant Others of Rape Victims." *Journal of Marital and Family Therapy*, 8(1):91-97. January, 1982.

Rothenberg, Robert E. (ed.), *The Plain-Language Law Dictionary*. New York: Penguin Books, 1981.

Russell, Diana E. *The Politics of Rape: The Victim's Perspective*. New York: Stein and Day, Publishers, 1975.

Ruth, Sheila. *Issues in Feminism: A First Course in Women's Studies*. Boston: Houghton Mifflin Company, 1980.

Sanders, William B. *Rape and Woman's Identity*. Beverly Hills, CA: Sage Publications, 1980.

Selkin, James. "Protecting Personal Space: Victim and Resister Reactions to Assaultive Rape." *Journal of Community Psychology*, 6(3):263-268. July, 1978.

Siegel, Larry J. *Criminology*. St. Paul, MN: West Publishing Co., 1983.

Silverman, Daniel C. "Sharing the Crisis of Rape: Counseling the Mates and Families of Victims." *American Journal of Orthopsychiatry*, 48(1):166-173. January, 1978.

Slovenko, Ralph (ed.), *Sexual Behavior and the Law*. Springfield, IL: Charles C. Thomas, Publisher, 1965.

Smart, Carol and Smart, Barry (eds.), *Women, Sexuality, and Social Control*. London and Boston: Routledge & Kegan Paul, 1978.

Stratton, John. "Law Enforcement's Participation in Crisis Counseling for Rape Victims." *Police Chief*, 43(3):46-49. March, 1976.

Sussman, Les and Bordwell, Sally. *The Rapist File*. New York and London: Chelsea House, 1981.

Warner, Carmen Germaine (ed.), *Rape and Sexual Assault: Management and Intervention.* Germantown, MD: An Aspen Publication, 1980.

Whiston, Sheila K. "Counseling Sexual Assault Victims: A Loss Model." *The Personnel and Guidance Journal,* 59(6):363-366. February, 1981.

Wickman, Peter and Whitten, Phillip. *Criminology: Perspectives on Crime and Criminality.* Lexington, MA: D.C. Heath and Co., 1980.

Wilson, Carolyn F. *Violence Against Women: An Annotated Bibliography.* Boston: G. K. Hall & Co., 1981.

Wolfgang, Marvin E. and Riedel, Marc. "Race, Judicial Discretion, and the Death Penalty." *The Annuals of the American Academy of Political and Social Science,* Volume 407:119-133. May, 1973.

Index